ILLUSTRATED LIBRARY OF COOKING

VOLUME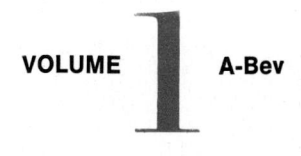

Four books in one: *a
primer of cooking that
includes both the terms and
techniques...a cornucopia
of classic American recipes
representing the East,
the South, the Midwest, the
Southwest and the West...a
treasury of party-starting
appetizers and hors d'oeuvres
...AND a bevy of beverages
for parties plain and fancy.*

ROCKVILLE HOUSE PUBLISHERS, INC.
ROCKVILLE CENTRE, NEW YORK 11570

VOLUME 1

Family Circle.

Illustrated Library of

COOKING

YOUR READY REFERENCE FOR A LIFETIME OF GOOD EATING

INTRODUCTION

In sixteen volumes, The Family Circle Library of Cooking is your ready reference for a lifetime of good eating. It contains more than 2000 pages, over 1000 color food illustrations and many thousands of what we consider the best recipes for you to use in your home—recipes that represent the finest in American regional cookery and favorite round-the-world classics, recipes that have been triple-tested in Family Circle's Kitchens by a staff of food experts.

The sixteen volumes are arranged alphabetically, not in the encyclopedic A-for-Apple-through-Z-for-Zucchini style, but in broad easy-to-use, *every-day* categories because *this* library is designed for the cook as much as the bookworm. Want a smashing new way to prepare hamburgers? Then reach for Volume III and Burger Bonanza. Little girl learning to cook? See Children's Hour, Volume V. Enjoy entertaining? Then it's Volume X and The Joy of Cooking for Others where you'll discover a trove of party menus and recipes. Concerned about nutrition? Read Here's Health, Volume IX. Counting Calories? You'll need Volume VI, Countdown on Calories.

You will need—*want*—all sixteen volumes, because each contains three or four specialized cookbooks—on breads, for example, cakes, casserole or campfire cooking. Each volume is jam-packed with recipes, with food facts and, we hope, *fun.* You'll find information on cooking equipment, a glossary of cooking terms, temperature tables, tips on how to measure ingredients and make recipe substitutions as well as a wealth of helpful hints on how to shop . . . prepare and serve meals for two, ten, twenty . . . use leftovers creatively . . . stretch the food dollar. There's up-to-the-minute information on nutrition and diets, on exciting new food products, on new cooking tests and techniques. Whole sections are devoted to do-ahead dinners, picnics and barbecues, family meals and festive meals, freezing and canning, and most contain hearty helpings of "back-to-scratch" recipes, reflecting modern woman's longing to get her hands into old-fashioned yeast doughs, to brew soups from soupbones, to make cakes that begin in bowls instead of boxes. But for the hurried (or harried), there are dozens of gourmet short-cuts that put today's dazzling array of instants and mixes to imaginative use.

Each one of the sixteen volumes has its own alphabetized recipe index, further broken down according to category — Soup, Meats, Vegetables, Desserts — so that you can see at a glance, just what recipes are in store. And as an additional service, there is a master index to all sixteen volumes in the final volume.

Together, the sixteen volumes add up to one of the most comprehensive and contemporary cooking libraries available today. Peruse them . . . *use* them. The world of good food is yours.

Arthur M. Hettich
Editor, Family Circle

(Left): Party food that is practically a meal: a giant ham, pinwheel platter of cold cuts, two salads and assorted breads and spreads. More ideas in Volume 1. (Below): From Volume 6, cool Molded Cantaloupe Cream.

Publishing Staff

Editor	Jean Anderson
Design and Layout	Margot L. Wolf
Production Editor	Donald D. Wolf
Photography Editors	Nye Willden
	John Tipton
Mechanicals	Morpad, Inc.

For Family Circle

Food Editor	Jane M. O'Keefe
Director Test Kitchen	Marie T. Walsh
Nutrition Editor	Ruth K. Mumbauer
Home Economist	Carole Burde Semel
Home Economist	Alyce W. Lienhard

Table of Contents

(Above): All together, a cornucopia of California fruits artfully arranged for a dessert platter. (Below): A parade of savory crêpes neatly sauced and all set for a buffet.

(Above): From Volume 6, Spareribs Kun Koki, sizzling on a hibachi, aglisten with rich glaze.

COUNTDOWN ON CALORIES
Common-sense Information on Dieting . . . Low-Calorie Menus and Recipes . . . Other Diet Helps . . . Height-Weight Charts for Men and Women

RECIPE INDEX

VOLUME 7

9

DESSERTS PLAIN AND FANCY
FAMILY CIRCLE'S Best Puddings, Custards, Gelatin and Fruit Desserts, Soufflés and Dessert Omelets, Crêpes, Dessert Sauces

DINNERS IN A DISH AND/OR A DASH
Inventive Casseroles and One-Dish Dinners

DO-AHEAD DINNERS
Meals To Cook One Day and Serve the Next

EASY-ON-THE-COOK BOOK
Busy-Day Dinners that Require Little Attention or Effort . . . Zip-Quick Meals

RECIPE INDEX

*What more festive for Christmas
than a succulent boneless ham,
carved in tissue-thin slices and
sparkly with sweet-sour glaze?
(Other menus for holiday feasting
are in Volume 9.)*

(Left): In its Easter finery, pink and smoky ham (Volume 9). (Below): Land of Plenty Preserved (Volume 10) is a short course on the art of making pickles, preserves, jams, jellies, and on canning fruits and vegetables.

VOLUME 10

Box lunches (Volume 11) can be movable feasts as this opulent open-face lobster sandwich proves.

VOLUME 11

VOLUME 12

Kielbasa makes Scandinavian Pea Soup a meaty main dish. More soups (Volume 15), more sausages (Volume 16).

VOLUME 13

VOLUME 14

VOLUME 15

VOLUME 16

A savory stew of lamb, limas and yellow squash.

13

SOME COOKING TERMS DEFINED; WHAT THE STARTER KITCHEN NEEDS: MEASURES, EQUIVALENTS AND OTHER TABLES; SOME PROFESSIONAL TIPS

To the experienced cook, there's nothing very mysterious about the language of food, those terms and techniques used daily in the art of cooking. But to the beginner, they are as foreign as French or Spanish. Defined here (or should we say "translated"?) are those cooking words and phrases that crop up most often in recipes. Also included in this section are some of the other basics of cooking: suggestions for equipping the beginning kitchen . . . tips on measuring . . . tables of equivalents and temperatures . . . information essential to every cook whether "all thumbs" or accomplished.

● ● ●

COOK'S CODE

Some cooking terms defined

A

à la: In the manner of; *à la Creole* means in the Creole style, *à la maison,* in the style of the house, "the house specialty."

al dente: Italian phrase meaning "to the tooth" used to describe spaghetti or other pasta at the perfect stage of doneness, tender but with enough firmness to be felt between the teeth.

Cooking terms illustrated (clockwise from upper left): compote *(stemmed dish for fruit compote, other desserts);* bombe *(fancy frozen mold);* glazed *melon balls.*

antipasto: Another Italian word, this one meaning "before the meal." Antipasto is the food, usually tart or biting, served before the main course.

aspic: A clear gelatin made from vegetable or meat broth.

au gratin: Topped with crumbs and/or cheese and browned in the oven or broiler.

B

bake: To cook, uncovered, in the oven by dry heat.

barbecue: To roast meat or other food, basting often with a highly seasoned sauce; also the food so cooked.

bard: To wrap meat or fowl in thin sheets of fat to prevent its drying out during roasting.

baste: To ladle drippings, marinade or other liquid over food as it roasts.

15

batter: A flour-liquid mixture thin enough to pour.

beat: To stir vigorously with a spoon or to beat with an egg beater or electric mixer.

beurre noir: French for "browned" (literally "black") butter.

bind: To add egg, thick sauce or other ingredient to a mixture to make it hold together.

bisque: A smooth, creamy soup, often with a shellfish base.

blanch: To scald quickly in boiling water.

blend: To mix two or more ingredients until smooth.

boil: To cook in boiling liquid.

bombe: Frozen dessert of two or more flavors layered in a fancy mold; also the mold itself.

bone: To remove bones.

bouillon: A clear stock made of poultry, beef or veal, vegetables and seasonings.

braise: To brown in fat, then to cook, covered, in a small amount of liquid.

bread: To coat with bread crumbs.

brochette: The French word for skewer.

broil: To cook under or on a grill by direct dry heat.

broth: A clear meat, fish, fowl or vegetable stock or a stock made of a combination of them.

brush: To apply melted butter, marinade or other liquid to food with a pastry brush.

C

canapé: A small, decorative open-face sandwich served with cocktails.

capon: A male chicken castrated while young so that it grows plump, fat and tender.

chapon: A cube of bread saturated with oil and garlic tossed with green salads to impart a delicate garlic flavor. It is removed before serving.

chop: To cut in small pieces.

clarify: To make stock, aspic or other liquid crystal clear by adding egg shell or egg white; also to clear melted butter by spooning off the milk solids.

clove of garlic: One segment of a bulb of garlic.

coat: To cover with flour, crumbs or other dry mixture before frying.

coat the spoon: Term used to describe egg-thickened sauces when cooked to perfect degree of doneness; when a custard coats a spoon, it leaves a thin, somewhat jelly-like film on a silver spoon.

coddle: To simmer gently in liquid.

combine: To mix together two or more ingredients.

compote: A mixture of sweetened, cooked fruits.

consommé: Clarified stock or bouillon.

core: To remove the core.

court bouillon: A delicate broth, usually fish and vegetable based, used for poaching fish.

cream: To beat butter or shortening alone or with sugar until fluffy.

crêpe: Very thin French pancake.

crimp: To flute the edges of a pie crust.

crisp: To warm in the oven until crisp.

croustade: A toast case used for serving creamed meats, fish, fowl or vegetables.

croutons: Small fried cubes of bread.

crumble: To break between the fingers into small irregular pieces.

cube: To cut into cubes.

cut in: To work shortening or other solid fat into a flour mixture with a pastry blender or two knives until the texture of coarse meal.

D

deep fry: To cook in hot deep fat.

demitasse: French for "half cup;" thus, small cups used for serving after-dinner coffee and the strong black coffee served in them.

devil: To season with mustard, pepper and other spicy condiments.

dice: To cut into small uniform pieces.

dot: To scatter bits of butter or other seasoning over the surface of a food to be cooked.

dough: Mixture of flour, liquid and other ingredients stiff enough to knead.

This checkerboard of canapés, dressed for a party, shows how irresistible the line-up of mini sandwiches can be.

(Left): More cooking terms illustrated: crêpes *(thin French-style pancakes) shown here with two of their American relatives.*

Demitasse

draw: To remove the entrails, to eviscerate. Also, to melt butter.

dredge: To coat with flour prior to frying.

dress: To eviscerate. Also, to add dressing to a salad.

drippings: The juices that cook out of food, usually meat, fish or fowl, during cooking.

drizzle: To pour melted butter, marinade or other liquid over the surface of food in a thin stream.

dust: To cover lightly with flour, confectioners' powdered sugar or other dry ingredient.

E

entrée: The main course of the meal.

eviscerate: To remove the entrails.

F

fillet: A thin boneless piece of meat or fish.

flake: To fork up a food, salmon or tuna, for example, until flaky.

flambé: A French word, meaning set afire.

flute: To crimp the edge of a pie crust in a fluted design.

fold in: To mix a light fluffy ingredient, such as beaten egg white, into a thicker mixture using a gentle over and over motion.

frappé: A mushy frozen fruit dessert.

French fry: To deep fry.

fricassee: To brown a food, then to cook, covered, with some liquid or sauce.

frizzle: To fry bacon or other thinly sliced meat over intense heat until the edges ruffle.

fromage: The French word for cheese.

frost: To cover with frosting; also to chill until frosty.

fry: To cook in a skillet in a small amount of fat.

G

garnish: To decorate with colorful and/or fancily cut small pieces of food.

giblets: the heart, liver and gizzard of fowl.

glacé: Candied.

glaze: To coat the surface of a food with honey, syrup or other liquid so that it glistens.

goulash: A stew.

granité: A mushy frozen dessert, water rather than milk or cream based.

grate: To cut into small pieces with a grater.

grease: To rub butter or other fat over the surface of a food or container.

grill: To cook on a grill.

grind: To put through a food chopper.

gumbo: A Creole stew made with tomatoes and okra and thickened with gumbo filé (ground dried sassafras leaves).

H

hors d´oeuvre: Bite-sized appetizers served with cocktails.

I

ice: To cover with icing. Also, a frozen water-based fruit dessert.

J

julienne: Food cut in uniformly long, thin slivers.

junket: A milk dessert thickened with rennet; also another name for rennet.

K

knead: manipulating dough with the hands until it is light and springy.

L

lard: creamy-white rendered pork fat; also, the act of inserting small cubes (lardoons) of fat in a piece of meat prior to roasting.

leaven: To add leavening (baking powder, baking soda or yeast) to a cake or bread to make it rise.

line: To cover the bottom, and sometimes sides, of a pan with paper or sometimes thin slices of food.

(Left): It's fromage *to the French,* cheese *to us and delicious in any language. Front and center, appropriately is Brie, known as "The Queen of Cheeses."*

lyonnaise: Seasoned in the style of Lyon, France, meaning with parsley and onions.

M

macedoine: A mixture of vegetables or fruits.

macerate: To let steep in wine or spirits.

marinade: The medium in which food is marinated.

marinate: To let food steep in a piquant sauce prior to cooking.

marzipan: Almond paste.

mash: To reduce to pulp.

mask: To coat with sauce or aspic.

meringue: Stiffly beaten mixture of sugar and egg white.

mince: To cut into fine pieces.

mix: To stir together.

mocha: Coffee-chocolate flavoring.

mold: To shape in a mold.

mousse: A rich creamy frozen dessert; also a velvety hot or cold savory dish, also rich with cream, bound often with eggs or if cold, with gelatin.

mull: To heat a liquid (often cider or wine) with spices so that it becomes spicy.

P

panbroil: To cook in a skillet with a very small amount of fat; drippings are usually poured off as they accumulate.

parboil: To boil until about half done; vegetables to be cooked *en casserole* are usually parboiled.

parch: To dry out or brown without the addition of any fat.

pare: To remove the skin of a fruit or vegetable.

pasta: The all-inclusive Italian word for all kinds of macaroni and spaghetti.

paste: A smooth creamy mixture of two ingredients.

pastry: A stiff flour-water-shortening dough used for pie crusts, turnovers and other dishes.

petits fours: Tiny fancily frosted cakes.

pilaf: Rice cooked in a savory broth, often with small bits of meat or vegetables, herbs and spices.

pipe: To squirt frosting, whipped cream, mashed potatoes or other soft mixture through a pastry tube.

pit: To remove pits.

plump: To soak raisins or other dried fruits in liquid until they plump up.

poach: To cook in simmering liquid.

pot roast: To brown, then to roast, covered, with some liquid.

pound: To flatten by pounding.

preheat: To bring oven or broiler to recommended temperature before cooking.

prick: To make holes over the surface of pastry using the tines of a fork.

Mousse Glacé

(Below): A new look for pilaf, *served* au gratin *in individual-size scallop shells.*

purée: To reduce food to a smooth velvety medium by whirling in an electric blender or pressing through a sieve or food mill; also the food so reduced.

R

ragout: A stew.

ramekin: A small individual-size baking dish.

reduce: To boil uncovered until quantity of liquid reduces.

render: To melt solid fat.

rennet: Material from a pig or calf's stomach used to curdle milk.

rice: To press through a sieve.

rissole: A small savory meat pie fried in deep fat.

roast: To roast in the oven by dry heat.

roe: The eggs of fish.

roll: To roll out with a rolling pin.

roux: A fat-flour mixture used in making sauces.

S

sauté: The French word for panfry.

scald: To heat a liquid almost to boiling, until bubbles form around edge of pan.

scallop: To bake small pieces of food *en casserole,* usually in a cream sauce.

score: To make criss-cross cuts over the surface of a food with a knife.

scrape: To remove vegetable peeling by scraping with a knife.

sear: To brown under or over intense heat.

seed: To remove seeds.

shirr: To cook whole eggs in ramekins with cream and crumbs.

shortening: The fat used to make cakes, pastries, cookies and breads flaky and tender.

shred: To cut in small thin slivers.

sieve: To put through a sieve.

sift: To put flour or other dry ingredient through a sifter. *Note:* Flour should always be sifted *before* it is measured.

simmer: To cook in liquid just below the boiling point.

singe: To burn hairs off fowl with a match.

skewer: Long metal or wooden pin on which food is impaled before being grilled; also the pin, itself.

skim: To remove fat or oil from the surface of a liquid or sauce.

sliver: To cut in long, thin pieces.

soak: To let stand in liquid.

spit: To impale food on a long rod and roast over glowing coals; also the rod, itself.

steam: To cook, covered, over a small amount of boiling water so that the steam circulates freely around the food, making it tender.

steep: To let food soak in liquid until liquid absorbs its flavor, as in steeping tea in hot water.

stew: To cook, covered, in boiling liquid.

stir: To mix with a spoon using a round and round motion.

stock: Meat, fowl, fish or vegetable broth.

strain: To put through a strainer or sieve.

stud: To stick cloves, slivers of garlic or other seasoning into the surface of a food to be cooked.

stuff: To fill the body cavity of fish or fowl.

T

thicken: To make a liquid thicker, usually by adding flour, cornstarch or egg.

thin: To make a liquid thinner by adding liquid.

timbale: A savory meat, fish, fowl or vegetable custard.

toss: To mix as for a salad by gently turning ingredients over and over in a bowl, either with the hands or with a large fork and spoon.

truss: To tie fowl into a compact shape before roasting.

W

whip: To beat until frothy or stiff with an egg beater or in an electric mixer.

Z

zest: Oily, aromatic colored part of the skin of citrus fruits.

Some Gourmet Gadgets *(clockwise from lower left):* Quiche pans, Mongolian hot pot, corn cutter, jar wrench, parsley cutter, skimmer, garlic basket, egg separator, paella pan, wok and ring for wok, garlic press, steamer basket, and for the ultimate gourmet, a "ravioli chef" for making ravioli.

WHAT THE STARTER KITCHEN NEEDS

21

Saucepans:
1-quart with lid
2-quart with lid
3-quart with lid
2 or 3-quart double boiler with lid

Skillets:
7" with lid
10" with lid

Kettles:
6-quart Dutch oven or heavy kettle with lid

Baking, Roasting Pans:
12" to 15" open roasting pan
13" x 9" x 2" loaf pan
9" x 5" x 3" bread pan
two 8" or 9" square cake pans
two 8" or 9" layer cake pans
9" or 10" tube pan
two cookie sheets

Casseroles, Bowls:
nest of mixing bowls
2 or 3-quart casserole with lid

Measurers:
measuring spoons
1-cup, 2-cup and 4-cup liquid measures
graduated dry measures

Thermometers:
meat
candy
deep fat
oven

Cutlery:
two paring knives

vegetable peeler
medium-size all-purpose knife
large slicing knife
large carving knife and fork
large chopping knife
four-sided grater
food grinder
kitchen shears
knife sharpener
large cutting board
Cooking Tools:
two wooden spoons
two rubber spatulas

large slotted spoon
ladle
long handled cooking fork
large and small strainers
flour sifter
funnel
rolling pin
pastry blender
pastry brush
pastry cloth and stockinette
cookie rack
two cake racks
pancake turner

narrow spatula
potato masher
Other Essentials:
egg beater
fruit juicer
can and bottle opener
corkscrew

SOME EQUIVALENT MEASURES

Pinch = less than ⅛ teaspoon
Dash = less than ⅛ teaspoon
3 teaspoons = 1 tablespoon
4 tablespoons = ¼ cup
5 tablespoons plus 1 teaspoon = ⅓ cup
8 tablespoons = ½ cup
16 tablespoons = 1 cup
1 fluid ounce = 2 tablespoons
½ pint = 1 cup
1 pint = 2 cups
1 quart = 4 cups or 2 pints
1 gallon = 4 quarts
1 peck = 8 quarts
1 bushel = 4 pecks

THE TEN MOST POPULAR CAN SIZES

22

CAN	APPROX. WT.	APPROX. CUPS
6-ounce	6 ounces	¾
Buffet	8 ounces	1
Picnic	10½ ounces	1¼
2 vacuum	12 ounces	1½ to 1¾
300	14 to 16 ounces	1¾
303	16 to 17 ounces	2
No. 2	1 pound, 4 ounces	2¼ to 2½
No. 2½	1 pound, 13 ounces	3¼ to 3½
46-ounce	3 pounds, 3 ounces	5¾ to 6
No. 10	7 pounds, 4 ounces	12 to 13

SOME EQUIVALENT AMOUNTS

½ stick butter or margarine = ¼ cup
1 stick butter or margarine = ½ cup
1 cup cream = 2 cups whipped cream
4-5 cups grated cheese = 1 pound
3-ounce package cream cheese = 7 table-
    spoons
3 cups cornmeal = 1 pound
1 small onion, chopped = ¼ cup
1 medium-size onion, chopped = ½ cup
1 large onion, chopped = 1 cup
1 orange = ⅓-½ cup juice
1 lemon = 2 tablespoons juice
1 orange rind, grated = about 1 tablespoon
1 lemon rind, grated = 1 teaspoon
2 cups uncooked rice = 1 pound
1 cup uncooked quick-cooking rice = 2 cups
    cooked rice
1 cup uncooked converted rice = 3-4 cups
    cooked rice
1 cup uncooked long grain rice = 4 cups
    cooked rice
1 cup uncooked wild rice = 3-4 cups cooked
    rice
1 cup uncooked noodles = 1¼ cups cooked
    noodles
1 cup uncooked macaroni = 2¼ cups cooked
    macaroni
1 pound nuts = about 2 cups nut meats
1 tablespoon cornstarch = 2 tablespoons flour
    (for thickening)
1¼ teaspoons arrowroot = 1 tablespoon flour
    (for thickening)
½ cup evaporated milk and ½ cup water = 1
    cup milk
¼ cup powdered whole milk and 1 cup water
    = 1 cup milk
3 tablespoons cocoa and 1 tablespoon short-

A space saver for every kitchen.

ening = 1 square of unsweetened chocolate
⅞ cup vegetable oil or shortening = 1 cup butter (for shortening)
¼ teaspoon soda and ½ teaspoon cream of tartar = 1 teaspoon baking powder
5 eggs = 1 cup
8-10 egg whites = 1 cup
12-15 egg yolks = 1 cup
2 cups sugar = 1 pound
4 cups sifted all-purpose flour = 1 pound
2 cups butter or margarine = 1 pound

TEMPERATURE TABLE

180° F.   Simmering (at sea level)
212° F.   Boiling (at sea level)

OVEN:

250°-275° F. Very Slow 400°-425° F. Hot
300°-325° F. Slow   450°-475° F. Very Hot
350°-375° F. Moderate

HOW TO MEASURE INGREDIENTS

In Dry Measures: These measuring cups, available in ¼, ⅓, ½ and 1-cup sizes, make it easy to fill the cup and level off ingredients flush with the rim (always use the edge of a spatula for leveling, never the broad side). Be sure to sift flour *before* measuring and to spoon *loosely* into the measure. Shortening, butter or margarine should be packed firmly into the measure and so should brown sugar.

In Liquid Measures: These glass measures have space at the top of the cup to allow for full measurement without spillage and lips for easy pouring. When measuring, set cup on a level surface, add needed amount, then check measurement at eye level by bending down, not by raising the cup.

In Measuring Spoons: Dip spoon into ingredient, then level off with the edge of a small spatula. To measure ½ tablespoon or ⅛ teaspoon, fill the tablespoon or ¼ teaspoon measure, level off, then divide amount in half horizontally.

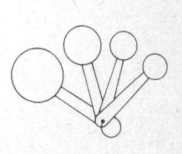

HOW TO MEASURE PANS

Good cooks know that for best results it pays to use the exact size pan, mold, or baking dish called for in a recipe. Here's how to be sure, if the size is not marked right on the utensil

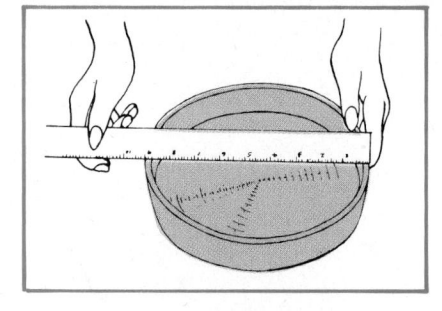

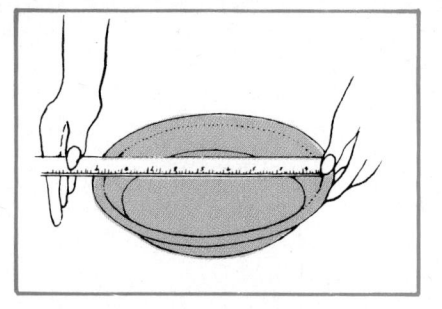

Layer-cake pans and pie plates— When selecting either of these bakers, measure diameter by placing ruler across top from inside to outside rim. Most family-size cake and pie recipes call for 8- or 9-inch sizes, although you'll find pie plates ranging all the way from 4 inches for individual tarts up to 12-inch jumbos

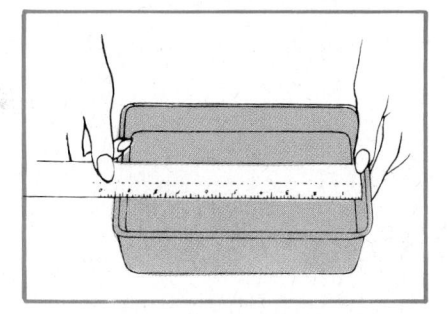

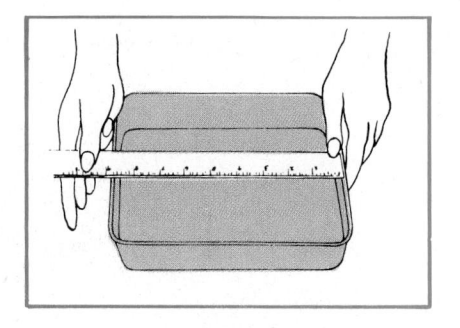

Loaf and square baking pans— Shown here is a 9-inch square, popular for bar cookies and candy. Measure 9x5x3 across the top, as pictured. Other choices in squares or oblongs are 8x8x2, 13x9 x2, and the familiar jelly-roll pan, 15x10x1

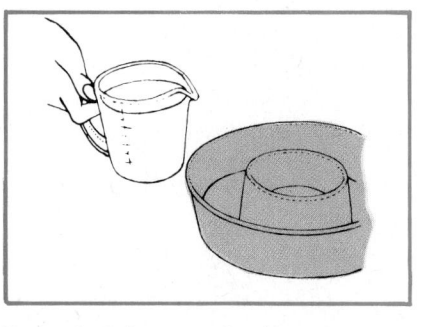

Fancy molds—What size you choose—and the same goes for casseroles—depends on the number of cups, pints, or quarts each will hold.

If you don't know, make this easy test: Fill a regular 1-, 2-, or 4-cup measure with water, then pour it into mold or dish

The dream of every gourmet cook—a heavy-duty, brass handled copper stock pot big enough to feed an army.

SOME PROFESSIONAL TIPS

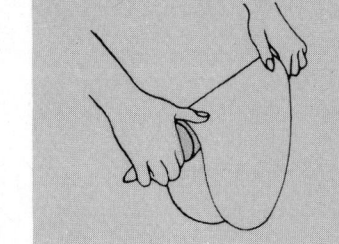

Every trade has its tricks—those certain little precautions or extra steps learned through experience—that help guarantee success. Add these good ideas to your list of cooking techniques.

1. For a quick trick in shaping your favorite drop cooky, just fill a pastry bag with dough, but don't use a metal tip. Press out just right amount of dough onto cooky sheet and flatten.

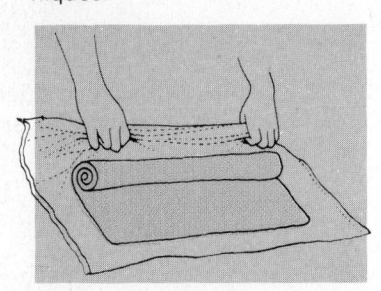

2. Jelly rolls are neater to roll if you use the towel trick: When roll is filled and ready, start first tight turn with your hand, then lift the towel higher and higher, and jelly roll will roll by itself.

3. To split cake layers, insert wooden picks at halfway mark all around layer. Ride blade of serrated knife on picks, cutting in toward center all around. Cut right across and through.

4. To handle that flaky pastry you have just rolled out, roll the dough up and over your rolling pin. Then lift it from the pastry board to the pie plate and gently unroll it into place.

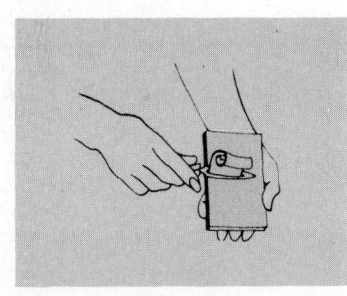

5. For jumbo chocolate curls for decorating, use your vegetable parer to help. Holding the parer flat, draw the blade across a plain chocolate candy bar. The curls will roll up very nicely.

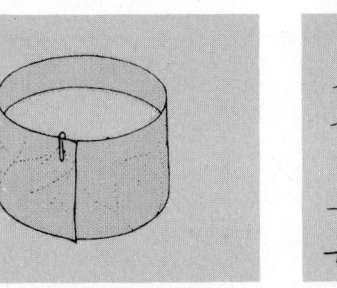

6. For a handsome effect when making your next cold soufflé, tie a collar of waxed paper around soufflé dish. When the soufflé is set and the paper is removed, the soufflé stands high.

7. To center gelatin mold on serving plate, smooth a few drops of water on plate with fingers; unmold gelatin as usual. The film of water will allow just enough slippage to move the mold.

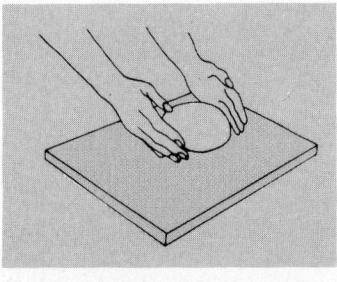

8. To roll pastry to an even round, form into a ball, flatten with hand, then start rolling from the center to the outside all around. Your pastry will be even and uniformly thick.

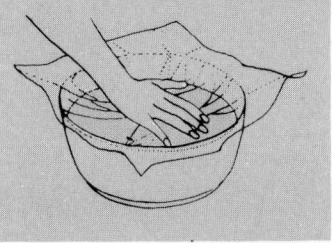

9. To keep cooked pudding and pie fillings nice and creamy, without that "skin" on top, press plastic wrap directly on hot filling. Cool, then refrigerate. Peel paper when set.

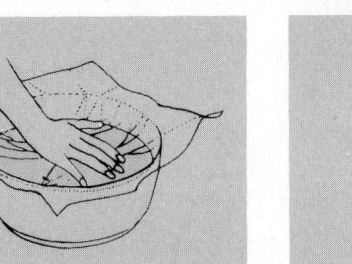

10. To frost cupcakes quickly, dip tops of cooled cupcakes into bowl of fluffy frosting. Give wrist a slight twist; quickly pull cupcake out. Frosting should be fairly soft for this.

Nifty storage trick: empty jars (ones popular foods are packed in); big jars are containers, small ones covers.

AMERICAN CLASSICS

AMERICAN CLASSICS:
FAVORITE RECIPES FROM THE EAST,
THE SOUTH, THE MIDWEST,
THE SOUTHWEST AND THE WEST

America's culinary heritage is varied and rich. In the East, particularly New England, seafood is king—lobster, hard and soft clams, scallops, mussels, oysters, cod, flounder and haddock. Yankee cooks have a way with them all. They have a way, too, with berries, particularly blueberries and cranberries which the Pilgrims found growing in abundance, and with the hearty, homely classics learned from the Indians—Boston Baked Beans, Johnnycake and Indian Pudding.

The South's gifts from the sea are blue crabs (at their best in Chesapeake Bay) and shrimp, the fattest and sweetest coming from the great crescent sweep of the Gulf Coast. Southern cooks are wizards at preparing the local catch, especially in Creole country where foods have a decidedly French-Spanish accent. They are adept, too, at cooking home-grown pork and fowl (is any ham lovelier than mellow, mahogany-hued Smithfield or any chicken more meltingly tender than Southern fried?). But where Southern cooks outdo themselves is in the dessert department (the whole South, it seems, has an insatiable sweet tooth). Peaches and strawberries, peanuts and pecans, sweet potatoes and yams are all stirred into too-good-to-be-true shortcakes, puddings and pies.

The Midwest, land of lyrical Indian-name states—Ohio . . . Iowa . : . Michigan . . . Minnesota . . . Nebraska . . . is corn and apple country. And what recipes there are! Apples and corn teamed with meats and vegetables or tucked into breads, dumplings, cobblers and pies. Sturdy fare descended from pioneer days.

In the Southwest, the vast ranchlands have produced a trove of beef and lamb recipes, robust cowboy fare, simply prepared and seasoned, counter-balanced by chilis and stews aflame with hot red and green peppers. It is a cuisine born of three heritages—American Indian, Spanish and English. A happy, hearty mix.

The West (Hawaii and Alaska included) is more than twice blessed: oceans of seafood (the Pacific's own varieties of crabs, clams, oysters and fin fish), orchards of avocados and citrus fruits, vineyards of grapes, farmlands overflowing with vegetables and salad greens. Salads, in fact, are the West's great specialty—green salads, fruit salads, vegetable salads, meat and fish salads. Salads to begin the meal, to end it, or salads that *are* the meal, itself.

And·now for the recipes—an Atlantic to mid-Pacific round-up of some of America's best.

29

American foods are as varied as the land that produces them. In the rugged Southwest (left), rough and ready barbecues are favored, especially if grilled outside.

THE EAST

New England Clam Chowder
Makes 6 to 8 servings

3 slices bacon, chopped
1 large onion, chopped (1 cup)
4 medium-size potatoes, pared and diced (3 cups)
3 cups water
1 teaspoon salt
¼ teaspoon pepper
2 cans (10½ ounces each) minced clams
1 bottle (8 ounces) clam juice
1 envelope non-fat dry milk (for 1 quart)
3 tablespoons flour
2 tablespoons minced parsley

1 Cook bacon until crisp in a large, heavy saucepan or Dutch oven. Remove bacon with slotted spoon; drain on paper toweling; reserve. Add onion to bacon drippings in saucepan; sauté until soft.
2 Add potatoes, 2 cups of the water, salt, and pepper; cover. Simmer, 15 minutes, or until potatoes are tender. Remove from heat.
3 Drain liquid from clams into a 4-cup measure; reserve clams. Add bottled clam juice and remaining cup of water.
4 Combine dry milk with flour in a small bowl; stir briskly into clam liquids in cup. Add to potato mixture in saucepan. Cook, stirring constantly, over medium heat, until chowder thickens and bubbles 1 minute.
5 Add clams; heat just until piping-hot. Ladle into soup bowls. Sprinkle with parsley and reserved bacon. Serve with pilot crackers, if you wish.

Manhattan Clam Chowder
Makes 6 servings

1 cup chopped onion
⅔ cup finely minced celery
2 teaspoons finely minced green pepper
1 clove of garlic, minced
2 tablespoons butter or margarine
1 cup diced potatoes
3 cups boiling water, salted lightly
3 fresh tomatoes peeled, seeded and diced
1 pint freshly opened clams, minced
   Salt and pepper
   Thyme
   Cayenne
1 teaspoon minced parsley
3 to 4 soda crackers, coarsely crumbled

1 Simmer the onion, celery, green pepper and garlic in butter for 20 minutes.
2 Add potatoes and water. Cook until the potatoes are tender.
3 Add tomatoes, clams and their juice, salt, pepper, thyme and cayenne to taste. Bring chowder to a boil; add chopped parsley, and pour soup into a tureen over the crackers.

Baked Stuffed Lobster
In some areas, you can buy ready-cooked lobsters to make fixing even speedier
Bake at 425° for 15 minutes. Makes 4 servings

4 small live lobsters, weighing about 1¼ pounds each
1 cup (2 sticks) butter or margarine, melted
2⅔ cups unsalted soda cracker crumbs
1 cup chopped parsley
2 teaspoons paprika
1 teaspoon salt

1 Drop live lobsters into a very large kettle of rapidly boiling salted water; cover. Cook over high heat 8 to 10 minutes. Lobsters will turn a bright red. Remove at once with tongs; drain; let cool enough to handle.
2 Place each lobster on its back and cut down middle from head to tail with scissors, being careful not to cut through hard shell of back. Press lobster open so it will lie flat. (If needed, simply crack shell of back in a few places.)
3 Lift out the pink coral (roe), if any, and green

Clam chowder as Manhattan likes it—with tomatoes.

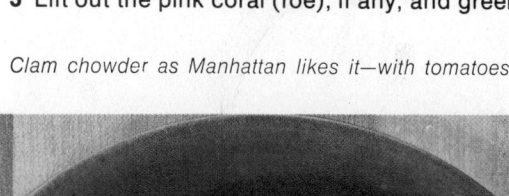

30

Stuffed Whole Fish comes to the table on a bed of carrots and peppers; Egg Sauce arrives in its own bowl.

tomalley (liver). Discard stomach sac or "lady" from back of head, black vein running from head to tail, and spongy gray tissue. Brush meat with some of the melted butter or margarine. Place lobsters on cooky sheets.

4 Mix cracker crumbs, parsley, paprika, and salt in a medium-size bowl; drizzle with remaining melted butter or margarine; toss lightly to mix. Pack into opened lobsters, dividing evenly.

5 Bake in hot oven (425°) 15 minutes, or until meat is hot and crumb topping is golden. Place on individual large serving platters; garnish each with water cress and lemon wedges, if you wish.

Stuffed Whole Fish

Proud presentation for the catch of your choice, appetizing inside and out
Bake at 350° for 1 hour. Makes 6 servings

- 1 whole sea bass, cod, or haddock, weighing about 3 pounds, dressed and boned
- 1 large onion, chopped (1 cup)
- ½ cup (1 stick) butter or margarine
- ½ teaspoon leaf sage, crumbled
- 2 teaspoons salt
- 6 slices white bread, cubed
- 1 egg, beaten
- 2 tablespoons lemon juice
- ¼ teaspoon pepper
  Egg Sauce (recipe follows)

1 Wash fish well in cold water; pat dry with paper toweling. Place in a greased large shallow baking pan.

2 Saute onion in 4 tablespoons of the butter or margarine until soft in a large frying pan; stir in sage and 1 teaspoon of the salt. Add bread cubes; toss to coat evenly; remove from heat. Stir in egg until well-blended. Spoon into cavity in fish.

3 Melt remaining 4 tablespoons butter or margarine in a small saucepan; stir in remaining 1 teaspoon salt, lemon juice, and pepper. Brush part over fish.

4 Bake in moderate oven (350°), brushing several times with remaining butter-lemon mixture, 1 hour, or until fish flakes easily.

5 Lift with wide spatulas onto a heated serving platter; spoon some of the *Egg Sauce** over fish; garnish platter with lemon wedges and parsley, if you wish. Serve remaining sauce separately.

EGG SAUCE—Hard-cook 3 eggs; shell and chop; set aside. Melt 4 tablespoons (½ stick) butter or margarine in a medium-size saucepan; stir in 4 tablespoons flour, ½ teaspoon salt, and ¼ teaspoon pepper; cook, stirring constantly, just until bubbly. Stir in 2 cups milk; continue cooking and stirring until mixture thickens and boils 1 minute; remove from heat. Stir in 1 tablespoon lemon juice; fold in chopped eggs. Makes about 2½ cups.

31

Herb-Baked Scallops

This natural delicacy doesn't need much enhancing—just some simple seasonings
Bake at 350° for 25 minutes. Makes 6 servings

- 2 pounds fresh sea scallops
  OR: 2 pounds frozen sea scallops, thawed
- ½ cup (1 stick) butter or margarine
- 3 tablespoons chopped parsley
- 1½ teaspoons leaf basil, crumbled
- 1 teaspoon salt
- ¼ teaspoon pepper

1 Wash fresh scallops in cold water; drain thoroughly between sheets of paper toweling.
2 Place in a single layer in a large shallow baking dish; dot with butter or margarine; sprinkle with parsley, basil, salt, and pepper.
3 Bake in moderate oven (350°) 5 minutes. Stir scallops to coat well with butter mixture. Bake 20 minutes longer, or until tender. Serve buttery sauce from dish over mashed or baked potatoes, if you wish.

Cape Cod Clam Pie

That clambake custom takes a surprising direction—baked in a pie!

Bake at 450° for 15 minutes, then at 350° for 30 minutes. Makes 6 servings

1 package piecrust mix
2 eggs
2 cans (10½ ounces each) minced clams
¾ cup milk
½ cup coarse unsalted soda cracker crumbs
1 teaspoon salt
¼ teaspoon pepper
2 tablespoons butter or margarine
1 teaspoon cold water

1 Prepare piecrust mix, following label directions, or make pastry from your own favorite two-crust recipe. Roll out half to a 12-inch round on a lightly floured pastry cloth or board; fit into a 9-inch pie plate.
2 Beat eggs well in a medium-size bowl; measure 1 tablespoon into a cup for Step 4.
3 Drain liquid from clams; measure out ¾ cup and stir into beaten eggs with clams, milk, cracker crumbs, salt, and pepper. Spoon into prepared pastry shell; dot filling evenly with butter or margarine.
4 Roll out remaining pastry to an 11-inch round; cut several slits near center to let steam escape; cover pie. Trim overhang to ½ inch; fold edges under, flush with rim; flute all around. Stir cold water into beaten egg in cup; brush over pastry.
5 Bake in very hot oven (450°) 15 minutes; lower oven temperature to moderate (350°). Bake 30 minutes longer, or until golden. Cool 15 minutes on a wire rack. To serve, cut in wedges.

Cape Cod Fish Balls

One of New England's most famous dishes is Cod Fish Balls. Few versions are finer than this one created at the Coonamessett Inn, Falmouth, Massachusetts.

Makes 6 servings, about 4 each

1 pound salt codfish
Instant mashed potatoes
Water
Salt
Butter or margarine
1 egg
2 egg yolks
Shortening or vegetable oil for frying

1 Place codfish in a large frying pan; cover with cold water. Heat to boiling; cover. Simmer 10 minutes, or until fish flakes easily; drain. Flake fish with a fork.
2 Prepare 4 cups instant mashed potatoes with water, salt, and butter or margarine, following label directions. (Omit milk called for.) Beat in egg and egg yolks; fold in codfish.
3 Melt enough shortening or pour vegetable oil into a deep-fat fryer or large saucepan to fill two thirds full; heat to 375°.
4 Drop cod mixture by tablespoonfuls into fat; fry, turning once, 1 minute, or until crispy-golden. Lift out with a slotted spoon; drain. Serve hot.

Pennsylvania Hot Pot

Smart-buy chuck, half moons of golden acorn squash, potatoes, and onions bake in a tomato-rich broth

Bake at 350° for 3 hours. Makes 6 to 8 servings

2 pounds beef chuck, cut in 1-inch cubes
¼ cup unsifted all-purpose flour
2 cups tomato juice
2 beef-bouillon cubes
1 tablespoon sugar
¼ cup finely chopped parsley
2 cloves of garlic, minced
3 teaspoons salt
¼ teaspoon pepper
4 medium-size potatoes, pared and sliced thin (4 cups)
8 small onions, peeled and quartered
1 acorn squash, split and seeded
2 tablespoons butter or margarine

1 Trim all fat from beef. Shake cubes, a few at a time, with flour in a paper bag to coat well.
2 Combine tomato juice, bouillon cubes, and

sugar in a small saucepan; heat, crushing cubes to dissolve, just to boiling.

3 Combine parsley, garlic, salt, and pepper in a cup.

4 Layer vegetables and meat into a 12-cup deep baking dish this way: Half of each of potatoes, onions, and beef, sprinkling each layer lightly with seasoning mixture. Repeat with remaining potatoes, onions, beef, and seasoning mixture.

5 Cut each squash half into 6 slices; pare; arrange on top. Pour hot tomato-juice mixture over; dot with butter or margaríne; cover.

6 Bake in moderate oven (350°) 3 hours, or until beef is tender.

Yankee Beef Platter
Makes 6 servings

1 boneless rolled chuck beef roast, weighing
    about 4 pounds
1 tablespoon instant minced onion
2 teaspoons salt
2 teaspoons sugar
½ teaspoon freshly ground pepper
⅛ teaspoon ground cloves
1 bay leaf
1 cup dry red wine
2 tablespoons vegetable oil
1 cup thinly sliced celery
2 cloves of garlic, sliced
1 can condensed onion soup
2 tablespoons flour
    Braised Leeks (recipe follows)

1 Pierce meat all over with a fork; place in a large glass or pottery bowl.

2 Sprinkle with onion, salt, sugar, pepper, and cloves. Add bay leaf and wine to bowl. Let stand, turning meat several times, 1 hour to season.

3 When ready to cook meat, remove from marinade; pat dry with paper toweling. Brown in oil in a heavy kettle or Dutch oven.

4 Stir in marinade, celery, garlic, and onion soup; heat to boiling; cover. Simmer, turning meat several times, 3 hours, or until tender. Remove meat to a carving board; keep warm.

5 Pour liquid into a bowl; let stand several minutes, or until fat rises to top, then skim off; remove bay leaf. Measure 2 tablespoons of the fat and return to kettle; blend in flour. Cook, stirring constantly, until bubbly. Stir in 1½ cups of the liquid; cook, stirring constantly, until gravy thickens and boils 1 minute.

6 Carve part of the roast into ¼-inch-thick slices. Arrange slices with rest of roast and *Braised Leeks** on a large serving platter. Add parslied potatoes and steamed whole carrots, if you wish. Serve gravy separately to spoon over all.

BRAISED LEEKS—Trim roots and about three fourths of the green tops from 2 bunches (4 to 5 in a bunch) leeks; split each leek lengthwise; wash well. Arrange pieces, cut side down, in a large frying pan. Add just enough water to cover; heat to boiling; cover. Simmer 5 minutes; drain; return to pan. Add 3 tablespoons butter or margarine and sprinkle with ½ teaspoon each salt and celery salt. Cook slowly, 5 minutes longer, or until leeks are tender. Makes 6 servings.

Red-Flannel Hash
Makes 4 generous servings

1 can (1 pound) julienne beets
2 cans (1 pound each) corned-beef hash
1 tablespoon instant minced onion

1 Drain beets, then pat dry between sheets of paper toweling.

2 Break up corned-beef hash with a fork in a large bowl; mix in beets and onion. Shape into 8 thick patties.

3 Sauté slowly, turning only once, until crusty-brown in a large frying pan. (No need to add any fat.) Serve hot with catsup or prepared mustard, if you wish.

Dried Corn Pudding
Bake at 350° for 45 minutes. Makes 8 servings

1 cup dried corn (from a 14-ounce package)
2 cups boiling water
2 teaspoons sugar
1 teaspoon salt
2 tablespoons butter or margarine
½ cup milk
4 eggs, separated
⅛ teaspoon pepper
    Paprika
    Chopped parsley

1 Combine corn and boiling water in a medium-size saucepan; cover; let stand 1 hour.

2 Stir in sugar, salt, and butter or margarine; heat to boiling; reduce heat; cover. Simmer 30 minutes; stir in milk; simmer 5 minutes longer. Drain liquid into a 1-cup measure. Add additional milk, if needed, to make ½ cup liquid.

3 Beat egg whites until stiff in a small bowl.

4 Beat egg yolks in a large bowl; stir in corn mixture, the ½ cup liquid, and pepper; stir in about ⅓ of the beaten egg whites, then fold in remainder. Pour into a buttered deep 6-cup baking dish. Set in a pan with 1 inch of hot water.

5 Bake in moderate oven (350°) 45 minutes,

33

or until the tip of a knife inserted 1 inch from edge comes out clean.

6 Remove from oven; let stand 5 minutes; sprinkle with paprika and parsley.

Note: To order dried corn by mail, request a price list from: John F. Cope Co., Manheim, Lancaster County, Pa. 17545.

Maple Glazed Squash And Parsnips
Makes 8 servings

    1 bunch medium-size parsnips (about 1½ pounds)
    2 small acorn squash (about ¾ pound each)
    1¼ cups maple syrup
    2 tablespoons butter or margarine
    1 tablespoon chopped parsley

1 Pare parsnips; quarter lengthwise, then cut into 3-inch pieces. Halve squash crosswise; scoop out seeds and stringy membrane; cut into ½-inch slices; do not pare.
2 Cook parsnips and squash, covered, in boiling salted water in a large skillet about 10 minutes, or until vegetables are almost tender; drain.
3 Heat maple syrup in same skillet; add butter or margarine, stirring until melted. Return parsnips and squash to skillet. Cook over medium heat, basting frequently (a bulb baster is best), about 15 minutes, or until vegetables are tender and richly glazed.

Parsnips and acorn squash, jeweled with maple sugar.

4 Remove squash with a slotted spoon; arrange slices, overlapping, around edge of a heated vegetable dish; spoon parsnips into center; drizzle remaining syrup over vegetables. Sprinkle with chopped parsley.

Boston Baked Beans
Bring out your big bean pot for cooking this one.

Bake at 300° for 5 hours. Makes 6 to 8 servings

    1 pound dried navy or pea beans
    1 medium-size onion, diced (½ cup)
    ½ cup molasses
    ½ teaspoon dry mustard
    ¼ cup firmly packed brown sugar
    1 teaspoon salt
    ¼ pound lean salt pork, diced

1 Pick over beans and rinse. Place in a large bowl; add water to cover; let stand overnight; drain.
2 Combine beans and onion in a large saucepan; add water to cover; heat to boiling; cover. Simmer 45 minutes, or until skins of beans burst when you blow on several in a spoon. Drain liquid into a small bowl.
3 Measure 1 cup of the bean liquid and combine with molasses, mustard, brown sugar, and salt in a bowl.
4 Layer half of the salt pork and all of the beans into an 8-cup bean pot or baking dish. Pour molasses mixture over top; add just enough more saved liquid to cover beans. Top with remaining salt pork, pressing down into liquid; cover.
5 Bake in slow oven (300°) 4 hours; uncover. Bake 1 hour longer, or until beans are deep brown, tender, and as dry as you like them. (After 2 hours baking, check beans, and if they seem dry, add more saved bean liquid to keep them moist.)

Cape Cod Cranberry Salad
Makes 8 servings

    1 can (about 9 ounces) pineapple tidbits
    1 package (3 ounces) red-cherry-flavor gelatin
    1 can (1 pound) jellied cranberry sauce
    ¼ cup lemon juice
    1 carton (8 ounces) cream-style cottage cheese
    ½ cup thinly sliced celery
    ½ cup coarsely broken walnuts
      Romaine

1 Drain syrup from pineapple into a 1-cup measure; add water to make 1 cup. Heat to boiling in a small saucepan; stir into gelatin in a medium-size bowl until gelatin dissolves. Beat in cranberry sauce and lemon juice. Chill 45 minutes, or until as thick as unbeaten egg white.
2 Stir in pineapple, cottage cheese, celery, and

34

New England's favorite, a huge bubbling pot of Boston Baked Beans, served forth here with a crisp criss-cross of bacon.

walnuts; spoon into a 6-cup mold. Chill several hours, or until firm (overnight is best).

3 When ready to serve, loosen salad around edge with a knife; dip mold *very quickly* in and out of hot water. Cover with a serving plate; turn upside down; gently lift off mold.

4 Garnish with romaine leaves. Serve plain, or with mayonnaise or salad dressing, if you wish.

Cranberry Chutney

For a change, chutney made with cranberries, fresh pears, and lemon peel

Makes about 3½ cups

1 package (1 pound) cranberries, stemmed
2 large pears, pared, quartered, cored, and diced
2 cups sugar
1 jar (4 ounces) candied lemon peel

1 Combine cranberries, pears, sugar, and lemon peel in a large saucepan. Heat, stirring constantly, to boiling; cover. Cook 5 minutes, or just until juice starts to flow; lightly skim off foam with a spoon.

2 Simmer, uncovered, 15 minutes, or until cranberries and pears are tender; pour into a bowl. Cool, then cover and chill.

Note: Chutney tastes equally good warm. Make it ahead, then reheat just before serving time.

Anadama Bread
Bake at 375° for 50 minutes. Makes 1 large round loaf

1½ cups water
½ cup yellow cornmeal
2 teaspoons salt
6 tablespoons butter or margarine
½ cup light molasses
2 envelopes active dry yeast
½ cup very warm water
6 cups sifted all-purpose flour
Cornmeal for topping

1 Heat water, cornmeal, salt, butter or margarine and molasses in medium-size saucepan until thick and bubbly. Pour into a large bowl; cool to lukewarm, about 45 minutes.
2 Sprinkle yeast into ½ cup very warm water in a cup. (Very warm water should feel comfortably warm when dropped on wrist.) Stir until yeast dissolves, then blend into cooled cornmeal mixture.
3 Beat in 2 cups of the flour until smooth. Stir in 3 more cups flour, 1 cup at a time, until dough is very stiff.
4 Turn out onto a lightly floured pastry cloth or board. Knead until elastic, about 10 minutes, using remaining cup of flour, as needed, to keep dough from sticking.
5 Place dough in a greased large bowl; turn to coat all over with shortening; cover with a towel. Let rise in a warm place, away from draft, about 1½ hours, or until double in bulk.
6 Punch dough down; knead in bowl a few times. Shape into a ball. Press into a greased 10-cup baking dish. Brush top with soft shortening; sprinkle with cornmeal.
7 Let rise again in a warm place, away from draft, 1 hour, or until double in bulk.
8 Bake in moderate oven (375°) 50 minutes, or until loaf is golden-brown, and gives a hollow sound when tapped. Remove from pan to a wire rack; cool. When cold, wrap in waxed paper, foil, or transparent wrap. Store overnight to mellow flavors, make slicing easier.

Johnnycake
Johnnycake wasn't named for Johnny Anyone. It's a corruption of Journey Cake, the sturdy cornmeal bread carried by early Yankee travelers. Nearly every good New England cook has a favorite recipe. The version that's brought fame to The Bank Cafe, Warwick, Rhode Island is this one.
Makes about 16 three-inch cakes

2 cups white cornmeal
1 teaspoon salt
¾ cup boiling water
1 cup milk

1 Combine cornmeal and salt in a medium-size bowl; stir in boiling water, then milk.
2 Drop batter, a heaping tablespoonful at a time, into a heated well-greased frying pan or onto a griddle; spread into a 3-inch round. Fry 1 to 2 minutes, or until underside is golden; turn; brown other side. Repeat with remaining batter, greasing pan before each baking.
3 Serve hot with melted butter or margarine and maple syrup.

Blueberry-Patch Muffins
Bake at 425° about 20 minutes. Makes 12 medium-size muffins

1 cup fresh blueberries
1 tablespoon sugar (for topping)
1 teaspoon grated lemon rind
2 cups sifted all-purpose flour
⅓ cup sugar (for batter)
3 teaspoons baking powder
1 teaspoon salt
1 egg, well beaten
1 cup milk
4 tablespoons (½ stick) butter or margarine, melted

1 Pick over blueberries; wash; spread on paper toweling to drain, then shake gently to dry well. Reserve for Step 4.
2 Combine 1 tablespoon sugar and lemon rind in cup. Reserve for Step 5.
3 Sift flour, ⅓ cup sugar, baking powder, and salt into medium-size bowl.
4 Combine egg, milk, and melted butter or margarine in small bowl; add all at once to dry ingredients; stir quickly and lightly just until liquid is absorbed (batter will be lumpy); gently fold in blueberries.
5 Spoon into 12 greased medium-size muffin-pan cups, filling cups ⅔ full; sprinkle reserved lemon-sugar over.
6 Bake in hot oven (425°) 20 minutes, or until golden-brown; remove from pan at once; serve hot with butter or margarine, or your favorite jelly or preserves.

Shoofly Pie
In Pennsylvania Dutch Country, women used to bake a special sticky-sweet pie to lure flies away from more cherished dishes. Shoofly Pie,

Blueberry-Patch Muffins, served steaming hot with lots of butter and jelly can't be beat for breakfast.

Anadama Bread, made of flour, cornmeal and molasses, is a 19th century recipe from Massachusetts.

it was called. Today the pie is a great Pennsylvania favorite, a specialty of many hotels and restaurants. The recipe below comes from the Shartlesville Hotel, Schartlesville, Pennsylvania.

Bake at 400° for 45 minutes. Makes 1 eight-inch pie

    1½ cups sifted all-purpose flour
    ½ cup sugar
        Dash of salt
    ¼ teaspoon ground cinnamon
     6 tablespoons shortening
    ½ cup molasses
    ½ cup hot water
    ½ teaspoon baking soda
     1 unbaked 8-inch pastry shell

1 Combine flour, sugar, salt, and cinnamon in a large bowl; cut in shortening with a pastry blender until mixture is crumbly. Measure out ½ cup and set aside for topping.
2 Mix molasses, water, and soda in a small bowl; stir into flour mixture until evenly moist. Pour into prepared pastry shell. Sprinkle the ½ cup crumb mixture over top.
3 Bake in hot oven (400°) 45 minutes, or until top springs back when lightly pressed with fingertip. Cool in pie plate on a wire rack. Cut in wedges.

Cranberry Tartlets
Bake shells at 400° for 10 minutes. Makes 3 dozen

     1 package piecrust mix
     2 large tart apples, pared, quartered, cored, and diced (2 cups)
     1 cup fresh cranberries, stemmed
    1½ cups sugar
    ⅛ teaspoon ground allspice
    ½ cup water
     2 tablespoons cornstarch
     1 cup cream for whipping
    ½ cup coarsely broken walnuts

1 Prepare piecrust mix, following label directions, or make pastry from your favorite double-crust recipe. Roll out, half at a time, to a rectangle, 14x10, on a lightly floured pastry cloth or board. Cut out 12 rounds with a 3-inch plain or scalloped cutter.
2 Fit each round into a tiny muffin-pan cup, pressing firmly against bottom and side. Repeat with remaining half of dough; reroll trimmings

and cut out to make 36 shells in all. Prick bottoms of shells with a fork.
3 Bake in hot oven (400°) 10 minutes, or until golden. Remove carefully from pans to wire racks; cool completely.
4 Combine apples, cranberries, sugar, all-spice, and ¼ cup of the water in a medium-size saucepan. Heat, stirring constantly, to boiling, then cook for 5 minutes.
5 Smooth cornstarch and remaining ¼ cup water to a paste in a cup; stir into cranberry mixture. Cook, stirring constantly, until mixture thickens and boils 3 minutes. Pour into a small bowl; cool, then chill.
6 Just before serving, beat cream until stiff in a small bowl. Spoon cranberry filling into tart shells; top each with a dollop of whipped cream; garnish with several walnut pieces.
    Day-before note: Make and bake tart shells. Cool; store carefully in a tightly covered container. Make cranberry filling and chill, ready to spoon into shells just before serving.

Boston Cream Pie
Bake at 350° for 25 minutes. Makes 8 servings

     1 package loaf-size yellow cake mix
        Egg
        Water
    ½ teaspoon lemon extract
     1 package (about 4 ounces) vanilla instant pudding mix
    1½ cups milk
     1 teaspoon vanilla
     1 square semisweet chocolate
     2 tablespoons butter or margarine
    ¼ cup 10X (confectioners' powdered) sugar

1 Prepare cake mix with egg, water, and lemon extract, following label directions. Pour into a greased and floured 9-inch round layer-cake pan.
2 Bake in moderate oven (350°) 25 minutes, or until top springs back when lightly pressed with fingertip. Cool in pan on a wire rack 10 minutes. Loosen around edge with a knife; turn out onto rack; cool completely.
3 Prepare pudding mix with milk and vanilla, following label directions.
4 Melt chocolate with butter or margarine in a small saucepan; remove from heat. Stir in 10X sugar and 1 teaspoon hot water until smooth.
5 Split cake layer; put back together, with vanilla filling between, on a large serving plate. Spread chocolate mixture over top, letting it drizzle down side. Chill until serving time. Cut into wedges.

Hot Apple Pandowdy
Bake at 350° for 50 minutes. Makes 10 servings

1¼ cups butter or margarine
⅔ cup sugar
1 egg, well-beaten
2½ cups sifted all-purpose flour
3 teaspoons baking powder
½ teaspoon salt
1 cup milk
3 cups sliced pared apples
¼ cup brown sugar
1 teaspoon ground cinnamon
2 cups Sweetened Whipped Cream

1 Cream butter or margarine and add sugar gradually. When well combined, mix in the egg.
2 Sift together flour, baking powder and salt and add alternately with the milk.
3 Spread apples in the bottom of a shallow, well-buttered ovenproof-china baking dish.
4 Mix together brown sugar and cinnamon and sprinkle over apples. Pour batter over the top, spreading it evenly.
5 Bake in moderate oven (350°) for about 50 minutes. Let stand for 10 minutes after removing from oven. To serve, invert on serving platter or serve directly from the baking dish. Pass *Sweetened Whipped Cream.**

SWEETENED WHIPPED CREAM—Beat 1 cup very cold cream for whipping until it is almost stiff. Fold in 1½ tablespoons 10X (confectioners' powdered) sugar and a few drops of vanilla. Makes 2 cups.

Note: A buttered baking pan or dish, 9x9x2, works equally well.

Cherry Cobbler
Here's the traditional deep-dish pie with plenty of juicy fruit under a blanket of golden pastry
Bake at 425° for 50 minutes. Makes 1 deep 8-inch pie

6 cups pitted tart red cherries
1¾ cups sugar
⅓ cup quick-cooking tapioca
1 teaspoon grated lemon rind
⅛ teaspoon salt
½ package piecrust mix
2 tablespoons butter or margarine

1 Place cherries in a large bowl; sprinkle with sugar, tapioca. lemon rind, and salt; toss lightly to mix. Let stand while making pastry.

2 Prepare piecrust mix, following label directions, or make pastry from your favorite single-crust recipe. Roll out to a 10-inch round on a lightly floured pastry cloth or board. Cut several slits near center to let steam escape. (Tip: To make sure pastry top will fit, turn your baking dish upside down over rolled-out pastry and measure, allowing an extra inch all around.)
3 Spoon cherry mixture into a 6-cup shallow baking dish; dot with butter or margarine. Cover with pastry; fold edge under, flush with rim; flute to make a pretty edge.
4 Bake in hot oven (425°) 50 minutes, or until pastry is golden and juices bubble up. Cool at least an hour on a wire rack. Serve in bowls, with plain cream, if you wish.

Yankee Fruit Cobbler
Easterners claim it tastes twice as good with apple and cranberry combined
Bake at 400° for 50 minutes. Makes 8 servings

6 medium-size apples
1½ cups sugar
⅓ cup flour
½ teaspoon ground nutmeg
2 cups cranberry-juice cocktail
2 cups biscuit mix
⅔ cup milk
1 teaspoon grated lemon rind

1 Pare apples, quarter, core, and slice into a shallow 8-cup baking dish. Combine 1¼ cups of the sugar, flour, and nutmeg in a small bowl; stir in cranberry juice until smooth. Pour over apples; cover.
2 Bake in hot oven (400°) 30 minutes, or until apples are tender.
3 Combine biscuit mix, 2 tablespoons of the remaining sugar, and milk in a medium-size bowl; stir just until evenly moist. Drop by tablespoonfuls in 8 mounds over hot apples. Mix remaining 2 tablespoons sugar and lemon rind in a cup; sprinkle over biscuits.
4 Bake 20 minutes longer, or until biscuits are golden. Serve warm.

Indian Pudding
The secret of this New England specialty is long slow baking
Bake at 325° for 3 hours. Makes 6 servings

5 cups milk
½ cup yellow cornmeal
½ cup sugar
½ cup molasses

39

4 tablespoons (½ stick) butter or margarine
1 teaspoon salt
1 teaspoon pumpkin-pie spice

1 Combine 2 cups of the milk with cornmeal and remaining ingredients in a large heavy saucepan. Heat slowly to boiling, then simmer, stirring often, 5 minutes, or until creamy-thick.
2 Pour into a buttered 8-cup baking dish; stir in 2 more cups milk.
3 Bake in slow oven (325°) 1 hour; stir in remaining 1 cup milk. Bake 2 hours longer, or until pudding sets. Serve warm with cream or ice cream, if you wish.

THE SOUTH

Maryland Stuffed Ham

Featuring a fresh color and flavor idea—greens tucked into deep cuts in meat
Bake at 325° for 3 hours. Makes 12 generous servings, plus enough for at least one bonus meal

1 fully-cooked ham, weighing about 12 pounds
1 package (10 ounces) fresh spinach
1 bunch green onions
1 bunch parsley
1 cup dry red wine
¾ cup honey
4 teaspoons cornstarch
2 tablespoons cider vinegar

1 Trim thick skin, if any, from ham. Make X-shape cuts, 3 inches deep and 1 inch apart, all over fat side with a sharp knife.
2 Trim stems from spinach and cut out any coarse ribs. Trim green onions and parsley; wash all greens well; dry on paper toweling. Chop all fine and mix well in a small bowl.
3 Press greens mixture into cuts, packing in well with your finger to fill openings. Place ham, fat side up, in a large shallow baking pan. Brush with part of the wine.
4 Bake in slow oven (325°), brushing several times with more wine, 2½ hours.
5 Stir honey into remaining wine; brush part of mixture over ham. Continue baking and brushing with remaining honey mixture 30 minutes,

A classic baked ham with a new twist, Maryland Stuffed Ham adds a splash of color to the dinner table.

or until top is richly glazed. Remove ham from pan and let stand about 20 minutes for easier carving.
6 Pour fat and juices from baking pan into a 4-cup measure; let stand a few minutes until fat rises to top; skim off fat. Add water to juices, if needed, to make 3 cups. Return to pan; heat to boiling.
7 Blend about 3 tablespoons cold water into cornstarch until smooth in a cup; stir into boiling liquid. Continue cooking and stirring, scraping baked-on juices from bottom and sides of pan, until sauce thickens and boils 3 minutes; stir in vinegar.
8 Turn ham meaty side up; cut a thin slice from bottom so it will stand flat. Place fat side up on platter. Cut a wedge-shape piece from shank end and lift out, then carve several slices and arrange at end of platter. Garnish platter with spinach leaves, green-onion curls, parsley, and spiced apple rings, if you wish. Serve sauce in separate bowl to spoon over meat.

Crumb-Topped Smithfield Ham

In Smithfield County in Virginia the hams have been cured in a special way to give them a flavor all their own. This is a ham to be enjoyed in thin, thin slivers with buttered hot biscuits or corn bread. Wonderful for a buffet party.
Bake at 350° for 1 hour. Makes 16 servings, plus leftovers

1 whole Smithfield ham, weighing about 14 pounds
  OR: 1 whole country-cured ham
½ cup light molasses
2 cups soft white bread crumbs (4 slices)

1 Soak ham overnight, or even 24 hours, in a large quantity of water. (If you have a free sink, that is the perfect place to soak the ham. This helps to remove some of the curing salt from the ham.)
2 Scrub the ham with a brush and rinse well to remove the pepper coating.
3 Place ham in a pan large enough to hold it and cover with cold water. (If this is impossible, fit ham, shank end up, in the largest roaster or kettle that you have and fill container with cold water. Wrap heavy duty foil around shank and up over kettle or roaster to cover.) Heat water to simmering, but do not boil. (Southerners say that boiling water drives the salt into the ham.)
4 Simmer ham, turning every 2 hours, 6 hours, or until a meat thermometer inserted into the thickest part of the ham reaches 160°.

41

5 Remove ham from water; cool. Refrigerate until ready to prepare.
6 Place ham in a shallow roasting pan; remove rind; trim fat; score remaining fat. Brush with part of the molasses.
7 Bake in moderate oven (350°) 30 minutes. Brush ham with remaining molasses and pat bread crumbs onto ham. Bake 30 minutes longer, or until crumbs are golden.
8 Cut ham into very thin slices, holding the carving knife almost parallel to the bone, starting at the shank end.

Burgoo

Stew ladled up for Kentucky Derby crowds makes servings by the dozen
Makes 12 servings

4 smoked ham hocks, weighing about 1 pound each
1 roasting chicken, weighing about 3 pounds
  Water
3 teaspoons salt
½ teaspoon cayenne
2 cups diced pared potatoes
2 cups diced pared carrots
2 large onions, chopped (2 cups)
1 package (10 ounces) frozen Fordhook lima beans
2 cups shredded cabbage
2 cups fresh corn kernels
2 cups thinly sliced celery
2 cups diced tomatoes
1 package (10 ounces) frozen whole okra
2 tablespoons Worcestershire sauce
1 cup diced green pepper
½ cup chopped parsley

1 Combine ham hocks and chicken in a kettle or roasting pan; add just enough water to cover. Heat to boiling; cover. Simmer 1½ hours, or until chicken is tender; remove from kettle. Continue cooking ham hocks 1 hour, or until tender; remove from kettle.
2 Let broth stand until fat rises to top, then skim off. Measure broth and return 12 cups to kettle. Stir in salt, cayenne, potatoes, carrots, onions, and lima beans. Heat to boiling; simmer 15 minutes.
3 While vegetables cook, remove skin from chicken and ham hocks; take meat from bones, discarding any fat; dice meat.
4 Stir cabbage, corn, celery, tomatoes, okra, and Worcestershire sauce into kettle; simmer 15 minutes, or until all vegetables are crisply tender. Stir in green pepper, parsley, and diced meats; heat just to boiling.

5 Ladle into soup plates or bowls. Serve with corn bread or crusty hard rolls, if you wish.

Country Pork and Black-Eyed Peas

Made for each other, this pair profits from long and leisurely cooking
Makes 4 to 6 servings, plus meat for another meal

1 package (1 pound) dried black-eyed peas
1 smoked pork picnic shoulder, weighing about 7 pounds
  Salt and pepper

1 Pick over peas, then rinse; place in a medium-size bowl. Add water to cover; let stand overnight; drain.
2 Place pork in a kettle; add water to cover. Heat to boiling; cover. Simmer 1½ hours.
3 Add peas to kettle; cover again. Simmer 1½ hours longer, or until pork and peas are tender. Remove pork from kettle; trim off skin and fat layers; slice about half of the pork ¼ inch thick.
4 Season peas to taste with salt and pepper; spoon onto a deep large platter; arrange pork slices over top. Wrap remaining pork and chill for another day.

Jambalaya

Rice from the fields of southwestern Louisiana is the backbone of this one-dish meat—a favorite as old as New Orleans itself.
Makes 8 servings

1 broiler-fryer (about 2½ pounds)
2 cups water
3 teaspoons salt
¼ teaspoon pepper
1 bay leaf
2 large onions, chopped (2 cups)
1 large clove of garlic, crushed
¼ cup (½ stick) butter or margarine
1 pound cooked ham, cubed
1 can (1 pound, 12 ounces) tomatoes
1 large green pepper, halved, seeded, and chopped
½ teaspoon leaf thyme, crumbled
¼ teaspoon cayenne
1 cup uncooked regular rice

1 Place chicken in a large kettle or Dutch oven; add water, salt, pepper, and bay leaf; bring to boiling; reduce heat; cover.
2 Simmer 45 minutes, or until chicken is tender; remove chicken from broth; reserve. When cool

42

enough to handle, remove meat from bones; cut into cubes; reserve.

3 Pour broth into a 2-cup measure; remove bay leaf; add water, if necessary, to make 2 cups; reserve.

4 Sauté onions and garlic in butter or margarine until soft in same kettle; add ham, tomatoes, green pepper, thyme, cayenne, and reserved chicken and broth. Heat to boiling; stir in rice; reduce heat; cover. Simmer, following rice label directions for cooking.

5 Serve in large bowls. Sprinkle generously with chopped parsley and serve with crusty French bread, if you wish.

Among the Deep South's gifts to good eating are the Gulf Coast's splendid shrimp and oysters, prepared as Oysters Rockefeller and Seafood Gumbo.

Oysters Rockefeller

An appetizer invented at Antoine's by Jules Alciatore in the 1850s—one so rich that it was named after the wealthiest man in the country.

Makes 6 servings

- 6 tablespoons butter or margarine
- ½ cup fine dry bread crumbs
- 2 cups fresh spinach leaves, washed and stemmed
- ½ cup parsley sprigs
- ½ cup diced celery
- 2 tablespoons diced onion
- 1 tablespoon Pernod liqueur

¼ teaspoon salt
3 drops liquid red pepper seasoning
18 large oysters on the half shell*
  Rock salt

1 Melt butter or margarine in a small saucepan; add bread crumbs; sauté for 1 minute, while stirring constantly.
2 Combine butter mixture, spinach, parsley, celery, onion, Pernod, salt, and pepper seasoning in electric blender container. Whirl at high speed, stopping blender to stir contents several times, until mixture is smooth. Pour into a small bowl; refrigerate until ready to use.
3 Arrange oysters on a bed of rock salt in six individual heatproof dishes, placing 3 in each dish. (Rock salt steadies oyster shells and retains heat.) Top each oyster with a tablespoonful of spinach mixture.
4 Broil 3 minutes, or just until topping is lightly browned and heated through. Serve at once.
  Note: If oysters in the shell are not available, place well-drained canned oysters in scallop shells or other small heat-proof serving dishes. Add topping and broil as above.

Baked Crab Meat Remick
Bake at 350° for 5 minutes. Makes 6 servings

3 cans (about 8 ounces each) crab meat
6 slices bacon, cooked and crumbled
1¾ cups mayonnaise or salad dressing
½ cup chili sauce
1 teaspoon tarragon vinegar
1 teaspoon dry mustard
½ teaspoon paprika
¼ teaspoon celery salt
  Few drops liquid red pepper seasoning

1 Drain crab meat; remove bony tissue, if any. Cut meat in chunks; place in 6 scallop shells or individual baking dishes; sprinkle with bacon. Place shells in a large shallow pan for easy handling. Heat in moderate oven (350°) 5 minutes while fixing topping.
2 Blend mayonnaise or salad dressing, chili sauce, vinegar, mustard, paprika, celery salt, and red pepper seasoning in a small bowl; spoon over hot crab mixture.
3 Broil, 4 to 5 inches from heat, 1 minute, or just until hot.

Crab Imperial, Chesapeake
Bake at 350° for 15 minutes. Makes 6 servings

4 cans (about 8 ounces each) crab meat
1 egg
⅔ cup finely diced green pepper
¼ cup finely diced pimiento
2 teaspoons dry mustard
2 teaspoons salt
¼ teaspoon white pepper
¾ cup mayonnaise or salad dressing
  Paprika

1 Drain crab meat; remove bony tissue, if any. Cut meat into chunks.
2 Beat egg in a medium-size bowl; stir in green pepper, pimiento, mustard, salt, pepper, and all but 2 tablespoons of the mayonnaise or salad dressing until well-blended. Fold in crab meat. Spoon into 6 ten-ounce custard cups or individual baking dishes. Spread top of each with 1 teaspoon of the remaining mayonnaise or salad dressing; sprinkle with paprika.
3 Bake in moderate oven (350°) 15 minutes, or just until hot.

Seafood Gumbo
Gumbo is the culinary pride of New Orleans and its greatest gift to American cuisine. This one is based on crab meat and oysters. (Use either fresh, or canned.)
Makes 8 servings

4 tablespoons (½ stick) butter or margarine
3 tablespoons flour
2 large onions, chopped (2 cups)
1 clove garlic, minced
1 can (1 pound, 12 ounces) tomatoes
1 can condensed chicken broth
2 cups water
1 teaspoon salt
1 tablespoon Worcestershire sauce
¼ teaspoon liquid red pepper seasoning
1 pound crab meat
  OR: 2 cans (7½ ounces each) crab meat
1 pint oysters
  OR: 3 cans (about 7 ounces each) oysters
2 tablespoons filé powder
  Creole Boiled Rice (recipe follows)

1 Make a roux (the flavor base for so many Creole dishes) by melting butter or margarine in a heavy kettle; stir in flour. Cook, stirring constantly, over low heat, until flour turns a rich brown, about 15 minutes.
2 Stir in onion and garlic. Cook, stirring often, until soft, about 10 minutes. Add tomatoes,

chicken broth, water, salt, Worcestershire sauce, and pepper seasoning. Cover kettle.

3 Simmer 15 minutes to develop flavors. Add crab meat and oysters with their liquor. Continue cooking, just until oysters are curled, about 5 minutes.

4 Sprinkle filé powder into gumbo and stir in to thicken broth. Serve in deep bowls over *Creole Boiled Rice*.

Note: Reheating with filé powder makes gumbo stringy; so always add it at last minute.

Creole Boiled Rice
Makes 8 servings

3 quarts water
2 tablespoons butter or margarine
1 tablespoon salt
2 cups uncooked regular rice

1 Heat water, butter or margarine, and salt to boiling in a large heavy saucepan. Stir in rice and heat to boiling.

2 Boil rice 15 minutes, or until tender. Drain rice in a large strainer. Pack into a buttered 8-cup bowl; cover bowl with foil.

3 Keep rice warm in a very low oven (250°) until ready to serve.

Cajun Shrimp Stew
Makes 6 servings

½ cup chopped celery
1 medium-size onion, chopped (½ cup)
1 clove of garlic, crushed
4 tablespoons (½ stick) butter or margarine
⅓ cup sifted all-purpose flour
½ teaspoon salt
½ teaspoon leaf thyme, crumbled
¼ teaspoon pepper

1 can (1 pound) tomatoes
1 can (about 14 ounces) chicken broth
1 can (8 ounces) minced clams
⅛ teaspoon liquid red pepper seasoning
1 can (about 1 pound) okra, drained
1 can (about 5 ounces) deveined shrimps, drained and rinsed
3 cups cooked rice

1 Sauté celery, onion, and garlic in butter or margarine until soft in a kettle. Stir in flour, salt, thyme, and pepper; cook, stirring constantly, until bubbly. Stir in tomatoes, chicken broth, clams, and liquid, and red pepper seasoning;

A Cajun classic—peppery okra-studded shrimp stew.

continue cooking and stirring until mixture thickens and boils 1 minute.

2 Add okra and shrimps; heat to boiling.

3 Ladle into a shallow serving bowl; spoon rice around edge. Or, spoon rice in mounds in center of soup plates; spoon shrimp mixture around rice.

Deviled Crab Bake
Zippy extras—mustard, lemon, and parsley—give zing to this partylike dish
Bake at 375° for 20 minutes. Makes 6 servings

1 tablespoon minced onion
3 tablespoons butter or margarine
3 tablespoons flour
1½ teaspoons dry mustard
½ teaspoon salt
2 cups milk
2 tablespoons lemon juice
Few drops liquid red pepper seasoning
2 tablespoons chopped parsley
2 cans (7½ ounces each) crab meat or 1 pound crab meat
4 hard-cooked eggs, shelled
1 cup coarsely crumbled soda crackers (12 crackers)

1 Sauté onion in butter or margarine just until softened in medium-size saucepan. Stir in flour, mustard, and salt; cook, stirring all the time, just until mixture bubbles. Stir in milk slowly; continue cooking and stirring until sauce thickens and boils 1 minute.

2 Remove from heat; stir in lemon juice, red pepper seasoning, and parsley.

3 Drain and flake crab meat, removing any bony tissue. Chop 3 eggs coarsely. (Save 1 for topping in Step 5.)

45

4 Stir crab meat, eggs, and ½ cup cracker crumbs into sauce mixture. Spoon into buttered shallow 6-cup baking dish or deep 9-inch pie plate; sprinkle remaining ½ cup crumbs over.
5 Bake in moderate oven (375°) 20 minutes. or until bubbly-hot. Slice saved egg; arrange on top; garnish with parsley, if you like.

Pork Chops Creole
Thick meaty chops bake on top a peppery blend of rice, kidney beans, and corn
Bake at 350° for 1 hour. Makes 6 servings

    6 rib or loin pork chops, cut ½ inch thick
    1 cup diced celery
    1 medium-size onion, chopped (½ cup)
    2 teaspoons chili powder
    1 can (about 1 pound) red kidney beans
    1 can (12 or 16 ounces) whole-kernel corn
    1 cup uncooked white rice
    1 can condensed tomato soup
    1 soup can of water
    1½ teaspoons salt
    1 teaspoon oregano
    ¼ teaspoon pepper
    ½ cup whole ripe olives

1 Brown pork chops in their own fat in large frying pan; remove and set aside; drain all but 2 tablespoons drippings from pan.
2 Sauté celery and onion until softened in same frying pan; stir in chili powder; cook 1 minute.
3 Stir in kidney beans and liquid, corn and liquid, rice, tomato soup, water, salt, oregano, and pepper; mix well. Heat to boiling.
4 Pour into greased 12-cup baking dish; arrange browned chops on top; cover with lid or foil, fastening around rim of dish to seal.
5 Bake in moderate oven (350°) 1 hour, or until rice and chops are tender. Garnish with ripe olives just before serving.

Dixie Pork and Sweets
Pork, apples, onions, and sweet potatoes make this Southern-style main dish
Bake at 350° for 2 hours. Makes 8 servings

    8 medium-size sweet potatoes (about 3
       pounds)
    3 pounds pork shoulder, cubed

    3 medium-size onions, sliced
    4 medium-size tart red apples, cored and
       sliced into rings
    2 tablespoons brown sugar
    3 tablespoons flour
    2 teaspoons salt
    1 teaspoon marjoram
    ¼ teaspoon pepper
    3 cups apple juice

1 Pare and quarter sweet potatoes. Cook in water just to cover in large saucepan 20 minutes, or until tender; drain.
2 Trim all fat from pork; brown, a few pieces at a time, in a little trimmed fat in large frying pan.
3 Arrange potatoes around edge of 12-cup baking dish; place half of meat in middle; top with a layer each of half the onion slices and apple rings; sprinkle with half the brown sugar. Repeat to make a second layer of meat and onions; overlap remaining apple rings around edge; sprinkle remaining brown sugar over.
4 Drain fat from frying pan. Measure and return 3 tablespoons to pan. Blend in flour, salt, marjoram, and pepper; slowly stir in apple juice. Cook, stirring constantly, until sauce thickens and boils 1 minute; pour over mixture in baking dish; cover; chill. Remove from refrigerator and let stand at room temperature 30 minutes before baking.
5 Bake in moderate oven (350°) 2 hours, or until meat is very tender.

Hoppin' John 'n' Ham
Cook 35 minutes in pressure cooker. Makes 8 servings

    1 pound dried black-eye peas
    1 shank-end smoked ham (about 4½ pounds)
    1 medium-size onion, diced (½ cup)
    2 teaspoons salt
    ¼ teaspoon pepper
    3 cups water
    2 cups uncooked white rice
    1 bunch green onions, trimmed and sliced

1 Soak peas overnight in water to cover generously (about 6 cups); drain.
2 Combine peas, ham, onion, salt, and pepper in a 6-quart pressure cooker; add the 3 cups water, being sure all peas are covered.
3 Secure cover, following manufacturer's directions; cook at 15 pounds pressure for 35 minutes, following manufacturer's directions.

Every Southern cook has her own favorite Southern Fried Chicken recipe. This crispy version is equally at home at picnics and posh parties.

Remove cooker from heat and allow pressure to drop of its own accord (about 10 to 15 minutes).
4 Meanwhile, cook rice, following label directions.
5 When pressure has dropped, remove cover. Place ham on carving board and cut off skin and fat. Cut into thick slices.
6 Add cooked rice to peas, tossing to mix well; spoon onto a heated deep platter; top with ham slices; sprinkle onions over top.

•

Southern Fried Chicken
Like any trick, a crisp crust is easy when you know how
Makes 6 servings

    2 broiler-fryers, weighing about 2 pounds
        each, cut up
    3 cups light cream or table cream
    2 cups sifted all-purpose flour (for chicken)
  2½ teaspoons salt
    ½ teaspoon pepper
        Shortening or vegetable oil
    1 tablespoon flour (for gravy)

1 Wash chicken pieces; pat dry. Place in a single layer in a large shallow dish; pour 1 cup of the cream over top; chill at least 20 minutes.
2 Shake chicken pieces, a few at a time, in a mixture of the 2 cups flour, 2 teaspoons of the salt, and ¼ teaspoon of the pepper in a paper bag to coat well. Dip each again in remaining cream in dish; shake again in flour mixture. (Double coating gives chicken its thick crisp crust.)
3 Melt enough shortening or pour enough vegetable oil into each of two large heavy frying pans to make a depth of 1½ inches; heat. Add chicken pieces, skin side down. Brown slowly, turning once, then continue cooking 30 minutes, or until crisp and tender. Remove to a heated serving platter; keep warm while making gravy.
4 Pour all drippings from frying pans into a small bowl; measure 2 tablespoonfuls and return to one pan. Stir in 1 tablespoon flour, remaining ½ teaspoon salt, and ¼ teaspoon pepper. Cook, stirring constantly, until bubbly. Stir in remaining 2 cups cream; continue cooking and stirring, scraping brown bits from bottom of pan, until gravy thickens and boils 1 minute. Serve separately to spoon over chicken.

47

Smothered Chicken

Chicken stays under cover to get moist and
tender, make memorable gravy

Bake at 350° for 1 hour. Makes 6 servings

    3 broiler-fryers, weighing about 2 pounds
        each, split
    ⅔ cup sifted all-purpose flour
    2 teaspoons salt
    ¼ teaspoon pepper
    6 tablespoons (¾ stick) butter or margarine
    1 medium-size onion, chopped (½ cup)
    2½ cups water

1 Wash chicken halves; pat dry. Shake with
mixture of ⅓ cup of the flour, 1½ teaspoons
of the salt, and pepper in a paper bag to coat
evenly.
2 Brown pieces, part at a time, in butter or
margarine in a large frying pan; place in a single
layer in a roasting pan.
3 Sauté onion until soft in drippings in frying
pan; stir in 1½ cups of the water and remaining
½ teaspoon salt. Heat, stirring constantly, to
boiling; pour over chicken; cover.
4 Bake in moderate oven (350°) 1 hour, or until
chicken is tender. Remove to a heated serving
platter and keep warm while making gravy.
5 Blend remaining ⅓ cup flour and 1 cup water
until smooth in a 2-cup measure. Heat liquid
in roasting pan to boiling; slowly stir in flour
mixture. Cook, stirring constantly, until gravy
thickens and boils 1 minute. Darken with a few
drops bottled gravy coloring, if you wish. Serve
separately to spoon over chicken.

Country Captain

Makes 8 servings

    2 broiler-fryers (about 2½ pounds each)
    ¼ cup unsifted all-purpose flour
    2 teaspoons salt
    ½ teaspoon pepper
    3 tablespoons vegetable oil
    1 large onion, chopped (1 cup)
    1 large green pepper, halved, seeded, and
        chopped
    1 large clove of garlic, crushed
    1 tablespoon curry powder
    1 can (1 pound) tomatoes
    ½ cup raisins or currants
        Hot cooked rice

1 Cut chicken into serving-size pieces.
2 Combine flour with 1 teaspoon of the salt and
¼ teaspoon of the pepper in a plastic bag.
Shake chicken, a few pieces at a time, in flour
mixture to coat; tap off excess.
3 Brown chicken, part at a time, in oil in a heavy

48

kettle or Dutch oven. Remove chicken; keep
warm.
4 Add onion, green pepper, garlic, and curry
powder to drippings remaining in kettle; sauté
until soft. Add tomatoes (breaking with spoon),
raisins, and reserved chicken; cover. Simmer
1 hour, or until chicken is tender. Arrange
chicken on a bed of rice. Spoon sauce over
top.

Brunswick Chicken

Meaty pieces of chicken, corn, and limas bake
flavorfully mellow in a peppy tomato sauce

Bake at 350° for 1½ hours. Makes 8 servings

    2 broiler-fryers (about 2 pounds each), cut up
    ½ cup sifted all-purpose flour
    1 envelope herb-salad-dressing mix
    ¼ cup shortening
    1 large onion, chopped (1 cup)
    1 tablespoon sugar
    2 cans (about 1 pound each) tomatoes
    1 package (10 ounces) frozen whole-kernel
        corn, cooked and drained
    1 package (10 ounces) frozen Fordhook lima
        beans, cooked and drained

1 Shake chicken in mixture of flour and salad-
dressing mix in paper bag to coat well. Brown,
a few pieces at a time, in shortening in large
frying pan; arrange in 12-cup baking dish.
2 Sauté onion in same frying pan; blend in any
remaining seasoned flour, and sugar; stir in
tomatoes. Heat to boiling, stirring constantly.
3 Spoon corn and lima beans around chicken
in baking dish; pour tomato sauce over; cover
with lid or foil; chill. Remove from refrigerator
and let stand at room temperature 30 minutes
before baking.
4 Bake in moderate oven (350°) 1½ hours, or
until chicken is tender.

Sally Lunn

High-rising yeast bread, faintly spiced, plus a
sprinkling of confectioners' sugar

Bake at 350° for 45 minutes. Makes 1 ten-inch
round coffeecake

    ¾ cup milk
    ⅓ cup granulated sugar
    1 teaspoon salt
    ½ cup (1 stick) butter or margarine
    1 envelope active dry yeast
    ¼ cup very warm water
    3 eggs, well-beaten
    1 teaspoon grated lemon rind

½ teaspoon ground mace
4 cups sifted all-purpose flour
10X (confectioners' powdered) sugar

1 Scald milk with granulated sugar, salt, and butter or margarine in a small saucepan; cool to lukewarm.
2 Sprinkle yeast into very warm water in a large bowl. (Very warm water should feel comfortably warm when dropped on wrist.) Stir until yeast dissolves; stir in cooled milk mixture, eggs, lemon rind, and mace.
3 Stir in flour until well-blended, then beat vigorously with a wooden spoon, scraping down side of bowl often, 100 strokes, or until dough is shiny elastic; cover with a towel.
4 Let rise in a warm place, away from draft, 1 hour, or until double in bulk.
5 Stir dough down; spoon into a greased 12-cup tube mold or 10-inch angel-cake pan; cover. Let rise again, 1 hour, or until not quite double in bulk.
6 Bake in moderate oven (350°) 45 minutes, or until bread is golden and gives a hollow sound when tapped. Remove from mold; cool on a wire rack. Sprinkle lightly with 10X sugar.

●

Bourbon Sweet Potatoes
Bake at 350° for 45 minutes. Makes 8 servings

4 pounds sweet potatoes or yams
½ cup (1 stick) butter or margarine, softened
½ cup bourbon
⅓ cup orange juice
¼ cup firmly packed light brown sugar
1 teaspoon salt
½ teaspoon apple-pie spice
⅓ cup chopped pecans

1 Scrub potatoes. Cook, covered, in boiling salted water to cover in a large saucepan, about

A new way to serve Sally Lunn, crowned with berries.

35 minutes, or just until tender. Drain; cool slightly; peel.
2 Place potatoes in a large bowl; mash. Add butter or margarine, bourbon, orange juice, brown sugar, salt, and apple-pie spice; beat until fluffy-smooth.
3 Spoon Into a buttered 6-cup baking dish; sprinkle nuts around edge.

4 Bake in moderate oven (350°) 45 minutes, or until lightly browned.

49

●

Colonial Corn Bread
Warm and golden, this bread is equally delicious spread with soft butter or homemade jelly.
Bake at 450° for 25 minutes. Makes 16 servings.

1½ cups yellow cornmeal
2 cups sifted all-purpose flour
2 tablespoons sugar

As Southern as magnolias, bourbon-spiked "sweets."

4 teaspoons baking powder
1 teaspoon salt
2 eggs
2 cups milk
4 tablespoons bacon drippings or shortening

1 Combine cornmeal, flour, sugar, baking powder and salt in a large bowl. Add eggs and milk. Stir to make a smooth batter; stir in bacon drippings.
2 Pour into two greased 8x8x2-inch baking pans.
3 Bake in hot oven (450°) 25 minutes, or until crusty and golden brown. Cool slightly in pans on wire racks; serve warm.

Spoon Bread

There are spoon breads and spoon breads but few are lighter or lovelier than this one from the Evans Farm Inn, McLean, Virginia.
Bake at 350° for 40 minutes. Makes 4 to 6 servings

5 eggs
4 teaspoons baking powder
¼ cup white cornmeal
1 tablespoon sugar
½ teaspoon salt
2 cups milk
2 tablespoons melted butter or margarine

1 Beat eggs with baking powder until foamy in a medium-size bowl.
2 Stir in cornmeal, sugar, salt, milk, and melted butter or margarine. Pour into a greased 6-cup baking dish.
3 Bake in moderate oven (350°) 40 minutes, or until puffed and golden. Serve hot in place of potatoes or bread.

Mississippi Shortcake

Sweetened strawberries and whipped cream layered between crisp biscuit "cookies"
Bake at 450° for 8 minutes. Makes 6 servings

2 cups biscuit mix
¼ cup sugar
⅔ cup milk
3 tablespoons melted butter or margarine
4 cups strawberries, washed, hulled, sliced, and sweetened to taste
1 cup cream, whipped

1 Combine biscuit mix and 2 tablespoons sugar in medium-size bowl (save remaining 2 tablespoons sugar for topping in Step 3). Stir in milk, following label directions for making biscuits.
2 Turn out onto lightly floured pastry cloth or board; knead lightly 10 times. Roll out to not more than ¼-inch thickness, *for biscuits must be thin;* cut out with floured 2-inch cutter to make 30 to 36 rounds.
3 Place on ungreased cooky sheet; prick all over with fork; brush with melted butter or margarine; sprinkle with saved 2 tablespoons sugar.
4 Bake in very hot oven (450°) 8 minutes, or until golden.
5 As soon as biscuits are done, put shortcakes together by layering strawberries and whipped cream between hot biscuits for each serving.

Georgia Peach Shortcake

Hot buttery-nut biscuit layers are heaped high with juicy peaches and snowy cream
Bake at 450° for 20 to 25 minutes. Makes 6 servings

3 cups sifted all-purpose flour
4 teaspoons baking powder
1 teaspoon salt
1 teaspoon cinnamon
½ cup firmly packed brown sugar
¾ cup (1½ sticks) butter or margarine
½ cup broken pecans
1 egg
¾ cup milk
8 large ripe peaches (about 2 pounds)
1 cup cream for whipping
¼ teaspoon almond extract

Mississippi Shortcake is made of biscuits, not cake.

50

1 Sift flour, baking powder, salt, and cinnamon into large bowl; stir in brown sugar. Cut in butter or margarine with pastry blender until mixture is crumbly; stir in pecans.

2 Beat egg slightly with milk in 1-cup measure; add all at once to flour mixture; stir with a fork until blended.

3 Grease backs of 2 nine-inch layer-cake pans; spread half the dough on each to within ½ inch of edge.

4 Bake in very hot oven (450°) 20 to 25 minutes, or until golden.

5 While shortcake bakes, peel, slice, and sweeten peaches. Whip cream with almond extract until stiff in small bowl.

6 Put hot shortcake layers together on serving plate with peaches and cream between and on top. Cut in wedges.

Virginia Pecan Pie

This Southern treat is sinfully rich. Serve it in small portions with a drift of softly whipped cream.

Bake at 350° for 45 minutes. Makes 1 nine-inch pie

½ package piecrust mix
4 eggs
1 cup sugar
½ teaspoon salt
1½ cups dark corn syrup
1 teaspoon vanilla
¼ cup all-purpose flour
1 cup pecan halves

1 Prepare piecrust mix, following label directions, or make pastry from your favorite single-crust recipe. Roll out to a 12-inch round on a lightly floured board; fit into a 9-inch pie plate. Trim overhang flush with rim. Press pastry to rim with the tines of a fork.

2 Beat eggs slightly in a medium-size bowl; blend in sugar, salt, corn syrup and vanilla; stir in flour. Pour into prepared shell; arrange pecan halves in pattern on top.

3 Bake in moderate oven (350°) 45 minutes, or until center is almost set but still soft. (Do not overbake, for filling will set as it cools.) Cool on wire rack. Serve with whipped cream, if you wish.

Sweet-Potato Pie

A tradition in the South, this dessert boasts a special rich pastry

Bake at 425° for 5 minutes, then at 325° for 40 minutes. Makes 1 nine-inch pie

Rich Pastry (recipe follows)
1 pound sweet potatoes
3 eggs
½ cup firmly packed dark brown sugar
½ teaspoon salt
½ teaspoon ground cinnamon
¼ teaspoon ground nutmeg
⅛ teaspoon ground ginger
Dash of ground allspice
1 tall can evaporated milk
1 cup cream for whipping
1 tablespoon molasses

1 Make *Rich Pastry.** Roll out to a 12-inch round on a lightly floured pastry cloth or board; fit into a 9-inch pie plate. Trim overhang to ½ inch; turn under, flush with rim; flute to make a stand-up edge. Chill while making filling.

2 Pare sweet potatoes and dice. Cook, covered, in boiling slightly salted water in a medium-size saucepan 15 minutes, or until tender; drain; shake in pan over low heat to dry. Mash, then beat until smooth with an electric beater.

3 Beat eggs slightly in a large bowl; stir in brown sugar, salt, spices, sweet potatoes, and milk. Pour into chilled pastry shell.

4 Bake in hot oven (425°) 5 minutes; lower oven temperature to slow (325°). Bake 40 minutes, or until center is almost set but still soft. (Do not overbake, for custard will set as it cools.) Cool pie on a wire rack.

5 When ready to serve, mix cream and molasses in a medium-size bowl; beat until stiff. Spoon onto pie.

RICH PASTRY—Combine 1½ cups sifted all-purpose flour and ½ teaspoon salt in a large bowl; cut in ¼ cup shortening and 4 table-

Not *for dieters, this devastatingly rich pecan pie.*

51

spoons (½ stick) butter or margarine with a pastry blender until mixture is crumbly. Sprinkle with 4 tablespoons cold water, 1 tablespoon at a time; mix lightly with a fork just until pastry holds together and leaves side of bowl clean.

Black Bottom Pie
Spicy crust holds layers of creamy chocolate and rum-flavor chiffon fillings
Bake crust at 300° for 5 minutes. Makes 1 ten-inch pie

  1¼ cups crushed gingersnaps
    6 tablespoons (¾ stick) butter or margarine, melted
    1 envelope unflavored gelatin
   ¼ cup cold water
    1 cup sugar
    1 tablespoon cornstarch
     Dash of salt
    2 cups milk
    4 eggs, separated
    2 squares unsweetened chocolate, melted
    1 teaspoon vanilla
    1 tablespoon rum flavoring
   ⅛ teaspoon cream of tartar
    1 cup cream, whipped

1 Mix gingersnap crumbs with melted butter or margarine in a small saucepan; press evenly over bottom and side of a 10-inch pie plate.
2 Bake in slow oven (300°) 5 minutes; chill.
3 Soften gelatin in water in a cup; set aside for Step 4.
4 Mix ½ cup of the sugar, cornstarch, and salt in a medium-size heavy saucepan; stir in milk. Cook, stirring constantly, over low heat until mixture thickens and boils 3 minutes. Beat egg yolks slightly in a small bowl; stir in a generous ½ cup of the hot cornstarch mixture, then stir back into saucepan. Heat, stirring constantly, just 1 minute. Remove from heat; stir in softened gelatin until dissolved.
5 Strain into a 4-cup measure, then spoon 1 cupful back into saucepan; blend in melted chocolate and vanilla. Pour into chilled crust; chill.
6 Stir rum flavoring into remaining custard; set measure in a pan of ice and water; chill, stirring often, at room temperature just until custard mounds slightly on a spoon.

52

7 While custard chills, beat egg whites with cream of tartar until foamy-white and double in volume in a large bowl; beat in remaining ½ cup sugar, 1 tablespoon at a time, until meringue forms soft peaks. Set bowl in ice and water; fold in chilled custard until fluffy-thick; spoon over chocolate layer. Chill 2 hours, or until firm. Top with whipped cream. To decorate with chocolate, shave thin strips from square of semisweet chocolate with vegetable parer.

THE MIDWEST

Iowa Corn Chowder
Makes 10 to 12 servings

    4 slices bacon, chopped
    1 large onion, chopped (1 cup)
    3 medium-size potatoes pared and diced (2 cups)
  2½ cups water
    1 teaspoon salt
   ¼ teaspoon pepper
    2 cans (about 1 pound each) whole kernel corn
    1 tall can evaporated milk
   ¼ cup sifted all-purpose flour
   ½ teaspoon paprika

1 Cook bacon until crisp in a large heavy saucepan or Dutch oven. Add onion; sauté until soft.
2 Add potatoes, 2 cups of the water, salt, and pepper; cover. Simmer 15 minutes, or until potatoes are tender. Remove from heat.
3 Stir in corn with can liquid, and evaporated milk. Blend flour with remaining ½ cup water; stir into chowder.
4 Cook, stirring constantly, over medium heat, until chowder thickens and bubbles 1 minute. Ladle into soup bowls. Sprinkle each with paprika. Serve with saltines, if you wish.

Country Ribs and Kraut
Spareribs turn crispy-brown, yet stay moist and tender when baked atop sauerkraut
Bake at 325° for 3 hours. Makes 6 servings

    2 cans (1 pound, 11 ounces each) sauerkraut
   ¼ cup firmly packed brown sugar
    4 to 5 pounds fresh spareribs
     Salt and pepper

Yeast breads are Midwestern mainstays—Kolache, coffee rings, even a transplanted Southern Sally Lunn.

1 Mix sauerkraut and brown sugar in large shallow baking pan.
2 Cut ribs into serving-size pieces; place on top of sauerkraut; sprinkle with salt and pepper.
3 Bake in slow oven (325°) 3 hours, turning ribs occasionally to brown and crisp on both sides. Arrange around edge of heated serving platter; spoon sauerkraut in middle.

●

Sausage and Apple Skillet Dinner
Makes 4 servings

1 *package hash brown potatoes with onions*
Water
Salt
Butter or margarine
2 *packages (8 ounces each) heat-and-serve sausages*
1 *can (1 pound) sliced apples*

2 *tablespoons sugar*
¼ *teaspoon ground cinnamon*
¼ *teaspoon salt*
¼ *teaspoon leaf sage, crumbled*

1 Prepare potatoes with water, salt, and butter or margarine, following label directions, in a medium-size skillet.
2 Heat sausages, following label directions, until golden-brown in a large skillet; move to one side of skillet. Add apple slices; sprinkle with sugar, cinnamon, salt, and sage; heat 5 minutes, or until tender and piping hot.
3 To serve, arrange potatoes, sausages, and apple slices on heated platter.

●

Iowa Boiled-Beef Dinner
Lean slices of beef with four vegetables make this invitingly hearty main dish
Makes 6 servings

53

3 to 4 pounds lean boneless beef chuck roast
1 tablespoon salt
2 peppercorns
1 bay leaf
6 cups water
6 small potatoes, scrubbed
6 yellow onions, peeled
6 medium-size carrots, pared and quartered
1 medium-size cabbage (about 2 pounds)

1 Place meat in large kettle; add salt, peppercorns, bay leaf, and water. Cover; heat to boiling; simmer 1½ hours.
2 Remove meat; let any fat rise to top of broth; skim; return meat to kettle.
3 Cut off a band of skin around middle of each potato; place potatoes, onions, and carrots around meat in kettle; simmer 1 hour longer, or until meat is fork-tender.
4 Cut cabbage into 6 wedges; arrange on top of meat and vegetables; cover. Cook 15 minutes, or until cabbage is tender.
5 Remove cabbage with slotted spoon and place at one side of heated large serving platter; place meat in center and carrots at other side. Place onions and potatoes in serving bowl.
6 Skim any last traces of fat from broth; remove bay leaf; spoon broth over vegetables. (Or chill all broth and use to make soup for another meal.)

Potato Pancakes
Potatoes cook tender inside, stay crisp and lacy around the edges
Makes 8 servings

6 medium-size potatoes
2 eggs
1 small onion, grated
1½ teaspoons salt
¼ teaspoon pepper
¼ teaspoon ground nutmeg
1 tablespoon flour
   Shortening

1 Pare potatoes; shred. (There should be about 3 cups). If you shred them ahead, place in a bowl and cover with cold water until ready to mix pancakes, then drain and dry well with paper toweling.
2 Beat eggs in a large bowl; stir in potatoes, onion, salt, pepper, and nutmeg. Sprinkle flour over top; stir in.
3 Melt enough shortening in a large heavy fry-

54

Descended from pioneer days, a rib-sticking boiled beef dinner that gets a meal together in one big pot.

ing pan to make a depth of ¼ inch; heat. Drop potato mixture, a scant ¼ cup for each cake, into hot shortening, flattening slightly with back of spoon to make thin cakes. Fry slowly, turning once, 3 to 5 minutes, or until crisp and golden. (If needed, add more shortening and reheat between batches.) Serve hot.

Scalloped Potatoes

Peppy cheese bakes melty and golden atop these moist creamy potatoes

Bake at 375° for 1 hour. Makes 6 servings

- 4 cups thinly sliced raw potatoes (about 6 medium-size)
- 2 tablespoons flour
- 1 teaspoon salt
- ⅛ teaspoon pepper
- 3 tablespoons butter or margarine
- 2 cups milk, scalded
- ½ cup shredded sharp Cheddar cheese

1 Layer about one third of the potatoes in a buttered 8-cup baking dish.
2 Combine flour, salt, and pepper in a cup; sprinkle about half over the potatoes; repeat layers, ending with potato slices on top; dot with butter or margarine.
3 Pour scalded milk over potatoes (milk should be just visible between top slices); cover.
4 Bake in moderate oven (375°) 45 minutes; uncover; sprinkle cheese evenly over top. Bake, uncovered, 15 minutes longer, or until potatoes are tender and cheese is melted. (If potatoes are to stand for a while before serving, pour an additional ½ cup scalded milk over just before adding cheese and baking for the last 15 minutes.

Kansas Corn Scallop

Hearty main dish gets its name and a lot of character from two kinds of corn

Bake at 325° for 1 hour. Makes 6 servings

- 1 can (12 or 16 ounces) whole-kernel corn
- 2 eggs
- 1 can (1 pound) cream-style corn
- 1 small can evaporated milk (⅔ cup)
- 4 tablespoons (½ stick) butter or margarine, melted
- 2 tablespoons instant minced onion
- ½ teaspoon salt
- ¼ teaspoon pepper
- 2 cups coarsely crushed soda crackers
- 1 package (12 ounces) process Swiss cheese, diced

1 Drain liquid from whole-kernel corn into a cup.
2 Beat eggs slightly in a large bowl; stir in corn and ¼ cup of the liquid, cream-style corn, evaporated milk, melted butter or margarine, onion, salt, and pepper; fold in crackers and diced cheese. Spoon into a greased 8-cup baking dish.
3 Bake in slow oven (325°) 1 hour, or until set. Let stand 5 minutes before serving.

Apple Streusel Muffins

Bake at 425° for 20 minutes. Makes 12 muffins

- 2 cups sifted all-purpose flour
- ½ cup sugar (for batter)
- 3 teaspoons baking powder
- 1 teaspoon salt
- ½ cup (1 stick) butter or margarine
- 1 medium-size tart apple, pared, quartered, cored, and diced (1 cup)
- 2 teaspoons grated lemon rind
- 1 egg
- ⅔ cup milk
- ¼ cup chopped walnuts
- 2 tablespoons sugar (for topping)

1 Sift flour, the ½ cup sugar, baking powder, and salt into a large bowl. Cut in butter or margarine with a pastry blender until mixture is crumbly. Measure out ½ cup for topping and set aside. Stir apple and 1 teaspoon of the lemon rind into mixture in bowl.
2 Beat egg well in a small bowl; stir in milk. Add all at once to apple mixture; stir lightly until evenly moist. Spoon into 12 greased large muffin-pan cups.
3 Blend reserved crumb mixture with remaining 1 teaspoon grated lemon rind, walnuts, and the 2 tablespoons sugar; sprinkle over batter in each cup.
4 Bake in hot oven (425°) 20 minutes, or until golden and tops spring back when lightly pressed with fingertip. Remove from cups to a wire rack. Serve warm with butter or margarine and jelly, if you wish.

55

Banana-Nut Bread

A loaf to bake today and serve tomorrow—fruit helps to keep it moist

Bake at 325° for 1 hour and 20 minutes. Makes 1 nine-inch long loaf

- 2⅔ cups sifted all-purpose flour
- 3 teaspoons baking powder
- 1 teaspoon salt

¼ teaspoon baking soda
½ cup (1 stick) butter or margarine
1 cup sugar
3 eggs
2 medium-size ripe bananas, peeled and mashed (about 1 cup)
¾ cup finely chopped pecans
2 teaspoons grated orange rind

1 Grease a loaf pan, 9x5x3; line bottom with waxed paper; grease paper.
2 Sift flour, baking powder, salt, and soda onto another sheet of waxed paper.
3 Cream butter or margarine with sugar until fluffy in a large bowl. Beat in eggs, one at a time, until fluffy again.
4 Stir in flour mixture, alternately with mashed bananas; fold in pecans and orange rind. Pour into prepared pan.
5 Bake in slow oven (325°) 1 hour and 20 minutes, or until golden and a wooden pick inserted in center comes out clean. Cool in pan on a wire rack 10 minutes. Loosen around edges with a knife; turn out onto rack; peel off waxed paper. Let cool completely. Wrap and store overnight for easier slicing.

Crumb Cake

Traditionally called cake, actually yeast bread with a streusel topper

Bake at 375° for 30 minutes. Makes 2 nine-inch squares

½ cup milk
¾ cup granulated sugar
1 teaspoon salt
1¼ cups (2½ sticks) butter or margarine
2 envelopes active dry yeast
½ cup very warm water
4 eggs, well-beaten
7 cups sifted all-purpose flour
½ teaspoon ground cinnamon
½ cup firmly packed brown sugar
    10X (confectioners' powdered) sugar

1 Scald milk with granulated sugar, salt, and ¾ cup of the butter or margarine in a small saucepan; cool to lukewarm.
2 Sprinkle yeast into very warm water in a large bowl. (Very warm water should feel comfortably warm when dropped on wrist.) Stir until yeast dissolves, then stir in cooled milk mixture and eggs.
3 Beat in 3 cups of the flour until smooth, then beat in another 2½ cups to make a soft dough.
4 Turn out onto a lightly floured pastry cloth or board; knead until smooth and elastic, adding only enough extra flour to keep dough from sticking.
5 Place in a greased large bowl; turn to coat all over with shortening; cover with a towel. Let rise in a warm place, away from draft, 1 hour, or until double in bulk.
6 Punch dough down; knead a few times; divide in half. Press each half into a greased baking pan, 9x9x2.
7 Combine remaining 1½ cups flour, cinnamon, and brown sugar in a medium-size bowl; blend in remaining ½ cup butter or margarine until mixture is crumbly. Sprinkle half evenly over dough in each pan; cover. Let rise again, 30 minutes, or until double in bulk.
8 Bake in moderate oven (375°) 30 minutes, or until golden. Cool in pans on wire racks 10 minutes. Remove from pans this way: Press a sheet of foil lightly over top of each square to hold crumbs in place; turn upside down and lift off pan; turn right side up. When cool, sprinkle with 10X sugar.

Apple Kuchen

Goes together fast to complement coffee perfectly, flatter guests in fine style

Bake at 350° for 45 minutes. Makes 1 nine-inch coffeecake

2 cups sifted all-purpose flour
2 teaspoons baking powder
½ teaspoon salt
¼ teaspoon pumpkin pie spice
1 cup firmly packed light brown sugar
½ cup (1 stick) butter or margarine
¼ cup dried currants
2 eggs
1 small can evaporated milk, (⅔ cup)
1 large tart apple, pared, cored, and sliced thin
2 tablespoons granulated sugar

1 Sift flour, baking powder, salt, and pumpkin-pie spice into a large bowl; stir in brown sugar.
2 Cut in 6 tablespoons of the butter or margarine with a pastry blender until mixture is crumbly. Measure out ½ cup and set aside for topping; stir currants into remainder.
3 Beat eggs slightly in a small bowl; stir in evaporated milk. Stir into flour mixture until well-blended. Spoon into a greased 9-inch pie plate.
4 Arrange apple slices, overlapping, in 2 circles on top. Sprinkle with the ½ cup reserved crumb mixture; dot with remaining 2 tablespoons butter or margarine; sprinkle evenly with granulated sugar.
5 Bake in moderate oven (350°) 45 minutes, or until firm in center. Cool 10 minutes on a wire rack; cut in wedges. Serve warm.

Banana-Nut Bread bakes into a rich brown loaf; with ½ cup minced candied fruits added, it's holiday-gay.

Apricot-Almond Crescents

Yeast dough in a most appealing form, with fruit and nuts rolled up inside

Bake at 350° for 20 minutes. Makes 2 large coffeecakes

¼ cup milk
1 cup granulated sugar
1½ teaspoons salt
¾ cup (1½ sticks) butter or margarine
2 envelopes active dry yeast
½ cup very warm water
3 eggs, beaten
5 cups sifted all-purpose flour
½ teaspoon ground cardamom
1 package (11 ounces) dried apricots, chopped fine
1 can (about 4 ounces) sliced almonds
1½ cups 10X (confectioners' powdered) sugar
1 tablespoon cold water

1 Scald milk with ½ cup of the granulated sugar, salt, and ½ cup of the butter or margarine in a small saucepan; cool to lukewarm.
2 Sprinkle yeast into very warm water in a large bowl. (Very warm water should feel comfortably warm when dropped on wrist.) Stir until yeast dissolves, then stir in cooled milk mixture and eggs.
3 Beat in 2 cups of the flour and cardamom until smooth, then beat in remaining flour to make a stiff dough.
4 Turn out onto a lightly floured pastry cloth or board; knead until smooth and elastic, adding only enough extra flour to keep dough from sticking.
5 Place in a greased large bowl, turning to coat all over with shortening; cover with a towel. Let rise in a warm place, away from draft, 1 hour, or until double in bulk. Punch dough down; knead a few times. Divide in half.
6 Roll out one half to a rectangle, 14x10. Melt remaining ¼ cup butter or margarine in a small saucepan; brush half over dough. Sprinkle with ¼ cup of the remaining granulated sugar and half of the apricots and almonds.
7 Roll up, jelly-roll fashion; place, seam side down, on a greased large cooky sheet; curve into a crescent. With scissors, cut outside edge of crescent, making cuts 1 inch apart almost to inner edge; separate cuts slightly.
8 Repeat rolling, filling, and cutting with remaining half of dough. Place on a second greased cooky sheet; cover. Let rise again 30 minutes, or until double in bulk.
9 Bake in moderate oven (350°) 20 minutes, or until golden. Cool on cooky sheets on wire racks 10 minutes; remove carefully with two wide spatulas.
10 Blend 10X sugar and cold water in a small

57

bowl to make a thick icing; spread over coffeecakes while warm.

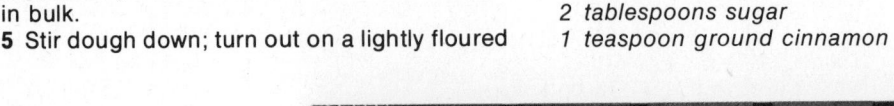

Kolache
Yeast rolls—sweet and shapely, plump with prune filling
Bake at 350° for 15 minutes. Makes 2 dozen rolls

½ cup milk
2 envelopes active dry yeast
½ cup very warm water
¾ cup (1½ sticks) butter or margarine
½ cup sugar
1 teaspoon salt
4 egg yolks
4½ cups sifted all-purpose flour
Prune Filling (recipe follows)

1 Scald milk in a small saucepan; cool to lukewarm.
2 Sprinkle yeast into very warm water in a large bowl. (Very warm water should feel comfortably warm when dropped on wrist.) Stir until yeast dissolves.
3 Beat butter or margarine with sugar, salt, and egg yolks until light and fluffy in large bowl of electric mixer. Stir in yeast mixture, cooled milk, and 2 cups of the flour. Beat 5 minutes at medium speed or 300 strokes by hand.
4 Stir in remaining flour to make a very soft dough; cover with a towel. Let rise in a warm place, away from draft, 1 hour, or until double in bulk.
5 Stir dough down; turn out on a lightly floured pastry cloth or board. Flour hands; knead dough several minutes; divide in half.
6 Roll out one half to a rectangle, 12x9; cut into 12 three-inch squares. Place 1 tablespoon *Prune Filling** in center of each. To shape each, fold one point over filling to cover, then fold opposite point over top; press to seal. (Filling will show at either end.) Place, 2 inches apart, on a greased large cooky sheet; cover.
7 Cut remaining half of dough into 12 even pieces; shape each into a smooth ball; place, 2 inches apart, on a second greased cooky sheet; cover.
8 Let all rise again 45 minutes, or until double in bulk.
9 Press large hollows in centers of round rolls with fingertips; place a tablespoonful *Prune Filling** in each.
10 Bake all in moderate oven (350°) 15 minutes, or until golden. Remove from cooky sheets; cool on wire racks.
PRUNE FILLING—Chop 1 package (12 ounces) pitted prunes; combine with 2 cups water and 2 tablespoons sugar in a medium-size saucepan. Cook slowly, stirring constantly, 15 minutes, or until very thick; cool. Stir in 2 teaspoons grated orange rind. Makes 1¾ cups.

Apple Cobbler Cake
Bake at 350° for 50 minutes. Makes 8 servings

6 medium-size tart apples, pared, quartered, cored, and sliced (6 cups)
2 tablespoons sugar
1 teaspoon ground cinnamon

The rolling and tabletop farmlands of the Midwest are among America's most beautiful, most bountiful food-producing areas.

58

1 package loaf-size yellow cake mix
½ cup (1 stick) butter or margarine, melted
   Light or table cream

1 Combine apples, sugar, and cinnamon in a large bowl. Sprinkle ¼ cup of the dry cake mix over top; toss until apples are evenly coated. Spoon into a buttered baking pan, 8x8x2; cover.
2 Bake in moderate oven (350°) 30 minutes; remove from oven.
3 Mix remaining cake mix and walnuts in a medium-size bowl; drizzle melted butter or margarine over top; toss until mixture forms large crumbs. Sprinkle evenly over partly cooked apple mixture.
4 Bake 20 minutes longer, or until topping is puffed and golden. Cool slightly. Serve warm with cream.

Golden Apple Turnovers
Makes 1 dozen

1 package piecrust mix
1 can (1 pound) pie-sliced apples, drained
3 tablespoons brown sugar
½ teaspoon ground allspice
   Shortening or vegetable oil for frying
   10X (confectioners' powdered) sugar

1 Prepare piecrust mix, following label directions, or make pastry from your favorite double-crust recipe. Roll out, half at a time, ¼ inch thick, on a lightly floured pastry cloth or board. Cut out 12 rounds with a 4-inch cooky cutter.
2 Toss apples with brown sugar and allspice in a medium-size bowl. Spread 2 tablespoonfuls apple mixture over half of each pastry round; fold other half evenly over filling; press around edges lightly with a fork to seal.
3 Melt enough shortening or pour vegetable oil into a large frying pan or deep-fat fryer to make a depth of 1 inch; heat to 350°.
4 Drop turnovers, a few at a time, into hot fat; fry, turning often, 3 to 5 minutes, or until golden; remove from pan with a slotted spoon and drain well on paper toweling. While still warm, sprinkle with 10X sugar; serve slightly warm.

Cinnamon Apple Cake
If you're lucky enough to have any left, reheat for a breakfast coffeecake treat
Bake at 350° for 30 minutes. Makes 12 servings

2 cups sifted all-purpose flour
2½ teaspoons baking powder
1 teaspoon salt
½ cup granulated sugar
½ cup shortening

2 eggs
½ cup milk
3 large apples, pared, quartered, cored, and cut in thick slices
½ cup firmly packed brown sugar
1 teaspoon mace
1 teaspoon grated lemon rind
2 tablespoons butter or margarine, melted

1 Sift flour, baking powder, and salt into large bowl; stir in granulated sugar; cut in shortening with pastry blender until mixture is crumbly.
2 Beat eggs slightly with milk in 2-cup measure. Stir into flour mixture until well-blended; pour into greased baking pan, 13x9x2. Arrange apple slices, overlapping slightly, in rows to cover top.
3 Combine brown sugar, mace, lemon rind, and melted butter or margarine in small bowl; sprinkle over apples.
4 Bake in moderate oven (350°) 30 minutes, or until wooden pick inserted in top comes out clean. Cut in squares and serve warm, plain or with ice cream or whipped cream, if you wish.

Apple Cobbler Pie
Serve this spicy teaser in bowls, for there are lots of juicy apples between two rich pastry layers
Bake at 400° for 30 minutes. Makes 6 servings

1 recipe Plain Pastry (recipe follows)
1 cup sugar
4 tablespoons flour
1 teaspoon pumpkin-pie spice
½ teaspoon salt
8 cups sliced, cored, pared apples (about 3 pounds)
2 tablespoons butter or margarine
1 tablespoon lemon juice
   Cream
   Cinnamon-sugar

1 Make *Plain Pastry**. Roll out half to an 8-inch round on lightly floured pastry cloth or board; fit into an 8-inch round 6-cup baking dish to line bottom.
2 Mix sugar, flour, pumpkin-pie spice, and salt in 2-cup measure. Sprinkle over apples in medium-size bowl; toss lightly to mix. Spoon into prepared baking dish; dot with butter or margarine; drizzle lemon juice over.
3 Roll out remaining pastry to a 10-inch round; cut several slits near center to let steam escape; cover pie. Fold edge under flush with rim; flute. Brush pastry all over with cream; sprinkle lightly with cinnamon-sugar.
4 Bake in hot oven (400°) 30 minutes, or until crust is golden and juices bubble up. Cool on

59

wire rack. Serve warm with cream or ice cream, if you like.

PLAIN PASTRY—Sift 1½ cups sifted all-purpose flour and 1 teaspoon salt into medium-size bowl; cut in ½ cup shortening with pastry blender until mixture is crumbly. Sprinkle about 4 tablespoons cold water over; mix lightly with a fork just until pastry holds together and leaves side of bowl clean. Makes enough for 1 eight-inch pie.

Rhubarb Cobblecake

Homey dessert of orange biscuits on spice-sparked fruit, to serve warm with cream
Bake at 425° for 25 minutes. Makes 6 servings

1⅓ cups sugar
2 tablespoons cornstarch
¼ teaspoon ground cloves
½ cup orange juice
½ cup (1 stick) butter or margarine
1½ pounds rhubarb, washed, trimmed, and cut in ½-inch pieces (about 5 cups)
2 cups sifted all-purpose flour
3 teaspoons baking powder
1 teaspoon salt
1 cup milk
1 tablespoon grated orange rind

1 Combine 1 cup of the sugar, cornstarch, and cloves in a large saucepan; stir in orange juice. Heat slowly, stirring, until sugar dissolves.
2 Stir in 2 tablespoons of the butter or margarine and rhubarb; heat to boiling; spoon into an 8-cup baking dish.
3 Sift flour, baking powder, ¼ cup of the remaining sugar, and salt into a large bowl; cut in remaining 6 tablespoons butter or margarine until mixture is crumbly. Add milk all at once; stir just until moist. (Dough will be soft.) Drop in 6 even mounds on top of rhubarb mixture.
4 Mix remaining sugar and orange rind in a cup; sprinkle over biscuits.
5 Bake in hot oven (425°) 25 minutes, or until topping is puffed and golden. Serve warm with cream, if you wish.

Seafoam Walnut Cake

Tops in the Midwest: Fluffy yellow cake dotted generously with black walnuts
Bake at 375° for 30 minutes. Makes 1 nine-inch triple-layer cake

3 cups sifted cake flour
3 teaspoons baking powder
½ teaspoon salt
1 cup (2 sticks) butter or margarine
2 cups sugar
4 eggs
1 teaspoon vanilla
1 cup milk
1 cup finely chopped black walnuts
1 jar (12 ounces) red-currant jelly
Seafoam Frosting (recipe follows)

1 Grease 3 nine-inch layer-cake pans; line bottoms with waxed paper; grease paper.
2 Sift cake flour, baking powder, and salt onto waxed paper.
3 Cream butter or margarine with sugar until fluffy in a large bowl. Beat in eggs, one at a time, until fluffy; stir in vanilla.
4 Stir in flour mixture, a third at a time, alternately with milk; fold in walnuts. Pour batter into prepared pans, dividing evenly.
5 Bake in moderate oven (375°) 30 minutes, or until centers spring back when lightly pressed with fingertip.
6 Cool in pans on wire racks 10 minutes. Loosen around edges with a knife; turn out onto racks; peel off paper; cool layers completely.
7 Put layers together with currant jelly on a serving plate; frost side and top of cake with Seafoam Frosting*. Decorate with additional chopped walnuts, if you wish.

SEAFOAM FROSTING—Combine 1½ cups firmly packed brown sugar, ¼ cup water, 2 unbeaten egg whites, 2 tablespoons light corn syrup, ¼ teaspoon salt, and 1 teaspoon vanilla in the top of a double boiler; beat until blended. Place over simmering water. Cook, beating constantly, with an electric or rotary beater, 5 minutes, or until mixture triples in volume and holds firm marks of beater; remove from heat. Makes enough to frost 1 nine-inch triple-layer cake.

THE SOUTHWEST

Chilled Tomato-Salad Soup

Like gazpacho, serve this appetizer cold with sunny hard-cooked eggs to sprinkle over
Makes 8 servings

1 envelope unflavored gelatin
1 tablespoon sugar
3 teaspoons salt
1½ cups water
1 can (about 2 pounds) Italian tomatoes

At home on the range, a giant joint of lamb turning on the spit, glistening underneath a barbecue glaze.

60

¼ cup olive oil or vegetable oil
2 tablespoons lemon juice
1 small cucumber, pared, quartered, and
    sliced thin
1 medium-size green pepper, seeded and
    diced
1 cup grated carrots
1 cup sliced radishes
¼ cup thinly sliced green onions
3 hard-cooked eggs, sieved

1 Mix gelatin, sugar, and salt in a small sauce-pan; stir in water. Heat, stirring constantly, just until gelatin dissolves; pour into a large bowl.
2 Place tomatoes in an electric-blender container; cover. Beat at high speed 1 minute, or until smooth. (Or mash tomatoes with a fork first, then beat slowly with an electric beater.)
3 Beat into gelatin mixture along with olive oil or salad oil and lemon juice until completely blended. Chill several hours, or until slightly thick.

Beef Tacos with Green Chili Salsa

The Southwest, as much Spanish by heritage as Anglo or American Indian, is famous for its peppery dishes. An especially good recipe is this one which helped make Tiffany's, a Cerrillos, New Mexico restaurant, popular in piñon and ponderosa country.
Makes 8 servings, 2 each

1 pound ground round steak
1 medium-size onion, chopped (½ cup)
2 tablespoons butter or margarine
1 can (8 ounces) tomato sauce
1 tablespoon soy sauce
1 tablespoon Worcestershire sauce
1 clove of garlic, minced
    Shortening or vegetable oil for frying
1 can (10 ounces) tortillas
1 cup shredded sharp Cheddar cheese
2 medium-size tomatoes, chopped
2 cups chopped romaine
    Green Chili Salsa (recipe follows)

1 Mix ground round steak and onion; shape into a large patty. Brown in butter or margarine in a large frying pan, 5 minutes on each side, then break up into chunks. Stir in tomato, soy, and Worcestershire sauces, then garlic; simmer 10 minutes. Keep hot.
2 Melt enough shortening or pour vegetable oil into a deep-fat fryer or large frying pan to a depth of 1 inch; heat to 375°. Drop tortillas, 1 at a time, into hot fat; heat 1 to 2 minutes. Using two pairs of tongs, pick up each tortilla and lift out, bending into a U shape; hold several

seconds until crisp; drain well on paper toweling.
3 Spoon beef mixture into each tortilla; sprinkle with shredded cheese; stand in a baking pan. Heat in hot oven (425°), 5 minutes, or until cheese ments.
4 Spoon chopped tomato, then romaine over cheese in each tortilla. Serve with *Green Chili Salsa**.

GREEN CHILI SALSA—Finely chop 1 large tomato, 1 medium-size Bermuda onion, 2 jalapenos (from a 4-ounce can) or green chili peppers, and 2 cloves of garlic. Combine in a medium-size bowl; stir in ½ teaspoon salt. Let stand at least 15 minutes to season.

Texas Tacos

Make and fill pancakes ahead, if you like, then chill—or even freeze—until you're ready to add the topping and bake
Bake at 325° about 30 minutes. Makes 6 servings

Filling
2 pounds ground beef
1 envelope onion-soup mix
1 can (1 pound, 2 ounces) tomato juice
1 cup catsup
¼ cup firmly packed brown sugar
2 tablespoons vinegar
2 tablespoons Worcestershire sauce
2 teaspoons salt

Pancakes
3 eggs
1½ cups milk
1 cup sifted all-purpose flour
1 teaspoon salt
½ cup yellow cornmeal
2 tablespoons melted butter or margarine

Topping
2 cups dairy sour cream
1 cup (¼ pound) freshly grated sharp Cheddar cheese
1 medium-size green pepper, cut in thin rings
    Cherry tomatoes

1 Make filling: Brown ground beef in large heavy frying pan with cover; stir in remaining filling ingredients; mix well. Cover; cook over low heat, stirring occasionally, 2½ hours, or until mixture is thick. (Long, slow cooking makes the meat mixture mellow and rich-tasting.)
2 Make pancakes: Beat eggs with milk in medium-size bowl; sift in flour and salt, then stir in corn meal and melted butter or margarine; beat just until smooth.
3 Heat a 7-inch heavy frying pan over low heat; lightly grease with butter or margarine. Pour in a scant ¼ cup batter at a time; tip pan to cover

There are as many chili recipes in the Southwest as there are cooks. Here's a particularly good version.

bottom completely. Bake until pancake top appears dry and underside is golden; turn; brown other side. Repeat, lightly greasing pan before each baking, to make 12 pancakes.

4 Spoon about ¼ cup filling onto each pancake as it is baked; roll up and place, seam side down, in double row in buttered shallow baking dish. (Save any remaining filling to use for the topping in Step 6. There should be about 1 cup.)

5 Keep pancake rolls warm in very slow oven (250°) until all are baked and filled. (Or, if made ahead, cover lightly and chill, or wrap and freeze until ready to complete dish.)

6 Make topping: Spoon sour cream down middle of pancake rows; sprinkle with grated cheese; spoon saved filling along edges of sour cream.

7 Bake in slow oven (325°) 30 minutes, or until top is bubbly and pancakes are heated through. (If pancakes have been chilled, increase baking time to 45 minutes; if frozen, to 60 minutes.) Garnish with thin green-pepper rings and tiny cherry tomatoes.

Chili
Makes 16 servings

½ pound dried pinto beans
3 cans (about 1 pound each) tomatoes
3 green peppers, seeded and chopped
2 tablespoons vegetable oil
4 large onions, chopped (5 cups)
3 cloves of garlic, minced
½ cup minced parsley
½ cup (1 stick) butter or margarine
3½ pounds ground beef
⅓ cup chili powder
2 tablespoons salt
1½ teaspoons pepper
1½ teaspoons ground cumin

1 Pick over beans and rinse. Place in a large bowl; add water to cover; let stand overnight; drain.

2 Place beans in a large kettle, add water to cover; heat to boiling; cover. Simmer about 45 minutes or until skins of beans burst when you

63

blow on several in a spoon. Add tomatoes and simmer 5 minutes. Set aside.

3 Sauté green peppers in the 2 tablespoons vegetable oil 5 minutes; add onions and cook until soft, stirring frequently. Add garlic and parsley.

4 In à large skillet melt the ½ cup butter or margarine and lightly brown ground beef; add beef to onion mixture, stir in chili powder and cook 10 minutes.

5 Add beef mixture to beans, stir in remaining ingredients, cover and simmer 1 hour. Remove cover and continue cooking for 30 minutes. Skim fat from top and serve.

Sombrero Chili

Favorite with a twist! Meat is cubes of chuck, simmered fork tender in tomato-rich sauce, then combined with beans, corn, and rice
Makes 8 servings

2 pounds lean boneless beef chuck, cut in 1-inch cubes
¼ cup sifted all-purpose flour
2 tablespoons chili powder
2 teaspoons salt
¼ teaspoon pepper
¼ cup shortening
1 large onion, chopped (1 cup)
2 cans (about 1 pound each) red kidney beans
2 cans (about 1 pound each) tomatoes
1 can (12 or 16 ounces) whole-kernel corn
2 tablespoons butter or margarine
2 cups hot cooked rice
1 cup grated Cheddar cheese (4 ounces)
1 can (4 ounces) pimientos, sliced
1 can (3 to 4 ounces) hot chili peppers

1 Shake beef cubes with flour, chili powder, salt, and pepper in a paper bag to coat well. Brown, a few at a time, in shortening in a kettle or Dutch oven; return all meat to kettle. Stir in onion; sauté 5 minutes longer, or until onion is soft. Spoon off any excess drippings; stir any remaining flour-seasoning mixture into pan.

2 Drain liquid from kidney beans and add to beef mixture; stir in tomatoes; cover. Simmer, stirring several times, 1½ hours, or until beef is tender. Stir in kidney beans; heat just to boiling.

3 To serve, drain corn and heat in butter or margarine in a small saucepan. Spoon hot chili into a heated 12-cup deep serving bowl or tureen; spoon corn in a layer in center; top with a cone of hot rice. Or, if you prefer, omit the butter or margarine and simply heat corn in the chili mixture. Serve the rice separately, doubling the amount to 4 cups so guests can spoon chili over generous servings.

4 Serve with grated cheese to sprinkle over and sliced pimientos and chili peppers.

Chili Enchiladas

Fill tortillas ahead, then spoon on topping and bake at the last minute
Bake at 350° for 30 minutes. Makes 8 servings

Filling
8 frankfurters (about 1 pound), sliced thin
1 medium-size onion, chopped (½ cup)
1 clove of garlic, minced
1 tablespoon salad oil
1 teaspoon chili powder
¼ teaspoon salt
1 can (8 ounces) tomato sauce
1 can (about 1 pound) red kidney beans

Tortillas
2 packages refrigerated plain or buttermilk biscuits

Topping
2 cans (8 ounces each) tomato sauce
1 cup chili sauce
2 large onions, chopped (2 cups)
1 cup grated Cheddar cheese (¼ pound)

1 Make filling: Sauté frankfurters, onion, and garlic in salad oil in medium-size frying pan 5 minutes, or just until onion is soft.

2 Stir in chili powder, salt, tomato sauce, and beans. Simmer 15 minutes.

3 Make tortillas: Separate refrigerated biscuits; roll each out to a thin 5-inch round on lightly floured pastry cloth or board.

4 Heat griddle or large frying pan over low heat. Bake biscuits, a few at a time, 1 to 2 minutes, or until tops are bubbly and undersides flecked with brown. Turn; bake 1 to 2 minutes longer.

5 As each biscuit is baked, spread with a scant ¼ cup filling; roll up and place, seam side down, in double row in buttered baking pan, 13x9x2.

6 Make topping: Combine tomato sauce, chili sauce, and onions in small saucepan; spoon half of mixture evenly over filled tortillas; sprinkle with cheese. Simmer remaining sauce, uncovered, 15 minutes, or until slightly thick.

7 Bake tortillas in moderate oven (350°) 30 minutes, or until bubbly-hot. Serve with remaining hot sauce to spoon over.

Note—To make ahead, bake and fill enchiladas; place in baking pan; cover with a damp towel; chill. Remove from refrigerator and let stand at room temperature 30 minutes; add

topping as in Step 6, and bake, following directions above.

Spitted Leg of Lamb
Makes 6 to 8 servings

1 leg of lamb, weighing about 6 to 7 pounds
Barbecue Sauce (recipe follows)

1 Wipe leg of lamb with damp paper toweling. Center the lamb on the spit, following manufacturer's directions. Place spit in position over medium coals. Brush *Barbecue Sauce** over meat. Start rotisserie.
2 Roast 2 hours and 45 minutes, basting frequently with remaining sauce, for medium-rare meat.

Cowboy Beef
Chunky short ribs bake in a zippy tomato-rich sauce. Gravy goes along as a bonus topper
Bake at 350° for 1½ hours, then at 400° for 30 minutes. Makes 4 servings

4 pounds beef short ribs
Instant unseasoned meat tenderizer
2 teaspoons chili powder
Whole cloves
1 large onion, peeled and sliced
1 can (about 1 pound) stewed tomatoes
1 teaspoon salt
⅓ cup orange marmalade
¼ cup vegetable oil
2 tablespoons flour
⅓ cup cold water

1 Trim any excess fat from short ribs. Moisten meat and sprinkle with tenderizer, following label directions; sprinkle with chili powder. Stud each piece with 2 or 3 whole cloves.
2 Place meat in a single layer in a large shallow baking dish; top with onion slices.
3 Press tomatoes through a sieve into a small bowl; stir in salt; spoon over meat mixture; cover.
4 Bake in moderate oven (350°) 1½ hours, or until meat is almost tender. Remove from oven; place meat on a rack in a large shallow pan. Raise oven temperature to hot (400°).
5 Strain liquid from pan into a small saucepan; measure out 2 tablespoonfuls and mix with orange marmalade and vegetable oil in a small bowl; brush over ribs.

6 Bake in hot oven (400°) 30 minutes, or until meat is tender and richly glazed.
7 While ribs bake, blend flour and water to a paste in a cup; stir into remaining liquid in saucepan. Cook, stirring constantly, until gravy thickens and boils 1 minute. Serve separately to spoon over ribs.

Laredo Beef
Zesty chili seasons the stew as well as the fluffy-light dumplings
Makes 6 servings

2 pounds lean boneless beef chuck
¼ cup sifted all-purpose flour
2 teaspoons salt
1 teaspoon chili powder
½ teaspoon ground cumin
¼ teaspoon pepper
1 large onion, chopped (1 cup)
1 can (12 or 16 ounces) whole-kernel corn
1 can (about 1 pound) red kidney beans
1 envelope instant beef broth
    OR: 1 beef-flavor bouillon cube
    Chili Dumplings (recipe follows)

1 Trim any fat from beef; cut beef into 1-inch cubes. Shake with flour, salt, chili powder, cumin, and pepper in a paper bag to coat well.
2 Melt enough fat trimmings in a kettle or Dutch oven to make 2 tablespoons drippings. Add beef cubes, part at a time, and brown; stir in onion; sauté, stirring several times, until slightly soft.
3 Drain liquids from corn and beans into a 4-cup measure; add water, if needed, to make 3 cups; stir into beef mixture with beef broth or the bouillon cube; cover. Heat to boiling.
4 Simmer 2 hours, or until beef is tender. Stir in corn and beans; heat to boiling again.
5 While vegetables heat, make *Chili Dumplings.** Drop batter by tablespoonfuls on top of boiling stew to make 12 mounds. Cook, uncovered, 10 minutes; cover. Cook 10 minutes longer, or until dumplings are fluffy-light.
    CHILI DUMPLINGS—Heat 1 tablespoon butter or margarine with 1 teaspoon chili powder until bubbly in a small saucepan. Measure 2 cups biscuit mix into a large bowl; add ¾ cup milk and chili-butter mixture all at once; stir with a fork just until evenly moist.

65

Barbecue Sauce
The cook's temperament makes a barbecue sauce what it is—hot, spicy, mild, according to occasion and mood. There is no hard and fast rule, but there are a thousand and one barbecue sauces. Do your own adjusting.
Makes about 3½ cups

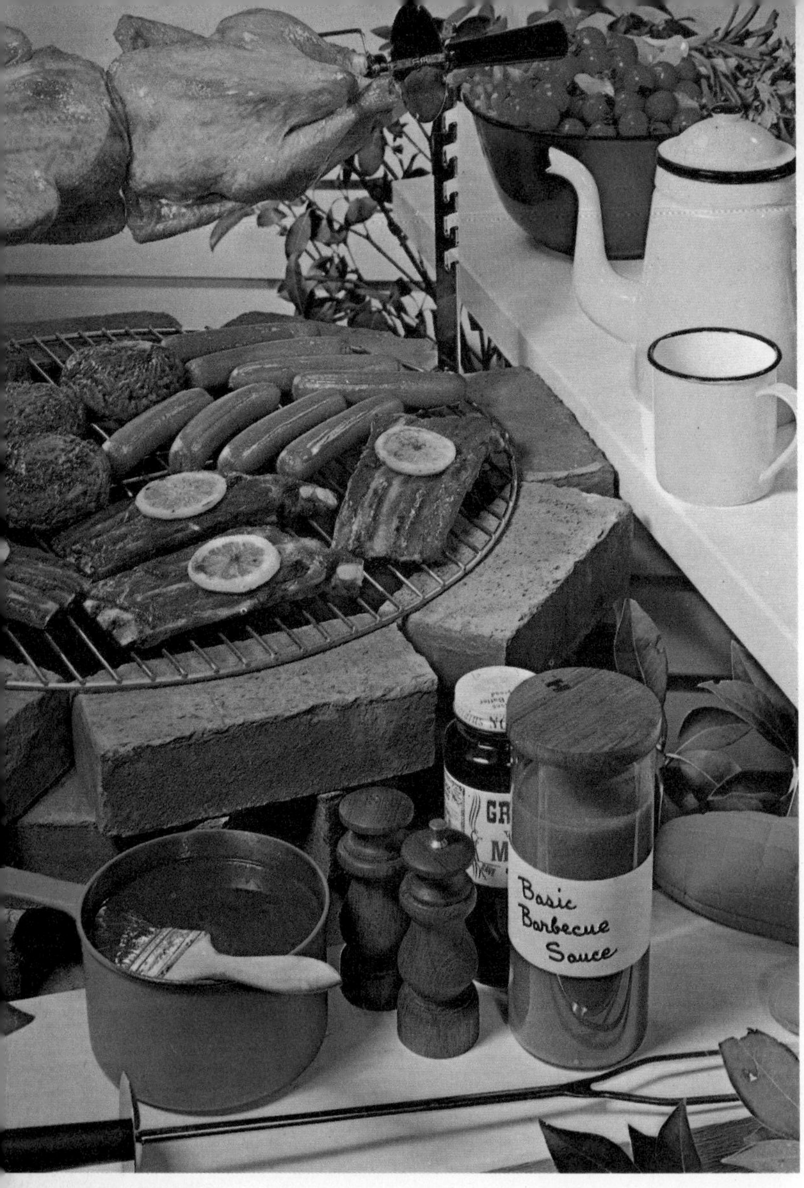

mustard, chili powder, salt, pepper, sugar, bay leaves, oregano, onion and garlic in a large saucepan. Bring to boiling; reduce heat; simmer, covered, for 15 minutes. Remove bay leaf. If the sauce is too thick, add a little water. For a smoother sauce, whirl in electric blender. Makes enough for 6 to 7 pounds of meat.

Deviled Lamb Ribs

Meat cooks crisp and brown over the coals and has a zesty mustard flavor
Makes 4 servings

    4 pounds breast of lamb
    ½ cup prepared mustard
    4 cloves garlic, minced
    2 teaspoons salt
      Chopped parsley

1 Trim any excess fat from lamb. Cut lamb, if needed, into pieces of 1 or 2 ribs each.
2 Mix mustard, garlic, and salt in a small saucepan.
3 Place ribs on grill about 10 inches from hot coals; brush with part of the mustard mixture.
4 Grill, turning and brushing several times with remaining mustard mixture, 1½ hours, or until meat is tender and richly browned. Before serving, sprinkle with chopped parsley and garnish with lemon wedges, if you wish.

Ranch-Style Chicken

Roast at 375° for 1½ hours. Makes 6 to 8 servings

    3 roasting chickens, weighing about 3 pounds
      each
    1 cup (2 sticks) butter or margarine
    ½ cup dry white wine
    1 teaspoon ground marjoram
    1 teaspoon garlic salt
    2 teaspoons salt
    ½ teaspoon pepper
      Water
    3 tablespoons flour

1 Remove giblets from body cavities of chickens. Wash chickens inside and out; pat dry. Place, breast sides up, in a large roasting pan.
2 Melt butter or margarine in a small saucepan; stir in wine, marjoram, garlic salt, salt, and pepper. Brush part over chickens.
3 Roast in moderate oven (375°), brushing several times with remaining butter mixture, 1½ hours, or until chickens are tender and golden. Remove to a heated serving platter; keep warm.

"Barbecue anyone?" A familiar cry in the Southwest.

66

    ½ cup butter or margarine
    1 cup vinegar
    1 cup water
    ½ cup catsup
    1 tablespoon Worcestershire sauce
    2 tablespoons lemon juice
    1 tablespoon dry mustard
    1 tablespoon or more chili powder
    1 teaspoon salt
    ½ teaspoon freshly ground pepper
    2 tablespoons sugar
    2 bay leaves
    ¼ teaspoon ground oregano
    1 large onion, minced
    2 garlic cloves, minced

Combine butter or margarine, vinegar, water, catsup, Worcestershire sauce, lemon juice, dry

4 Pour liquid from roasting pan into a 2-cup measure. Let stand several minutes until fat rises to top, then skim off. Add water to liquid, if needed, to make 2 cups. Return to pan; heat to boiling.

5 Blend flour with a little water to a paste in a cup; stir into boiling liquid. Cook, stirring constantly, until gravy thickens and boils 1 minute. Carve chickens; serve with gravy.

Chili Corn
Makes 6 to 8 servings

1 large onion, chopped (1 cup)
4 tablespoons (½ stick) butter or margarine
3 cans (12 or 16 ounces each) whole-kernel corn, drained
2 tablespoons chopped green chili peppers (from a 4-ounce can)
1 teaspoon salt
1 can (1 pound) sliced carrots

1 Sauté onion in 2 tablespoons of the butter or margarine until soft in a medium-size frying pan.

2 Stir in remaining butter or margarine, corn, chili peppers, and salt. Cook, stirring often, 15 minutes, or until lightly browned.

3 While corn browns, heat carrots in their liquid to boiling in a small saucepan; drain.

4 Spoon corn mixture into a serving bowl; overlap carrot slices around edge.

Squaw Corn
Makes 6 servings

5 medium-size ears sweet corn
1 small green pepper, halved, seeded, and chopped
1 small onion, chopped (¼ cup)
3 tablespoons butter or margarine
1 teaspoon salt
  Dash of pepper

1 Husk corn and remove silks; cut kernels from cobs. (There should be about 3 cups.)

2 Sauté green pepper and onion in butter or margarine until soft in a large frying pan. Stir in corn, salt, and pepper; cover.

3 Cook slowly, stirring once or twice, 10 minutes, or until corn is tender. Spoon into a heated serving bowl.

Rodeo Bean Roundup
Barbecue beans, chick peas, and corn take on a smoky tang

Bake at 400° for 1 hour. Makes 6 servings

1 can (about 1 pound) chick peas
1 can (12 or 16 ounces) whole-kernel corn
2 cans (1 pound each) barbecue beans
½ teaspoon leaf thyme, crumbled
6 slices bacon
½ small green pepper, seeded and diced

1 Drain liquids from chick peas and corn into a medium-size bowl. Combine peas, corn, beans, thyme, and ½ cup of the vegetable liquid in a bowl; spoon into a shallow 6-cup baking dish.

2 Bake in hot oven (400°) 30 minutes; lay bacon slices on top.

3 Bake 30 minutes longer, or until beans are bubbly hot and bacon is crisp. Sprinkle with diced green pepper.

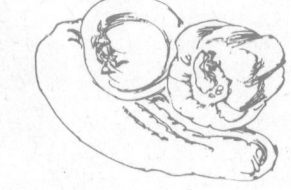

Chili-Bean Salad
Makes 6 servings

2 teaspoons chili powder
¼ cup olive oil or vegetable oil
2 tablespoons vinegar
2 teaspoons sugar
¼ teaspoon salt
2 cans (about 1 pound each) kidney beans, drained
1 large green pepper, diced (1 cup)
1 small Bermuda onion, diced (1 cup)
1 cup pitted ripe olives, halved
2 tablespoons catsup
1 tablespoon mayonnaise or salad dressing
1 small head of iceberg or leaf lettuce
1 package (8 ounces) sliced process American cheese

1 Heat chili powder in olive oil or vegetable oil in small saucepan about 2 minutes to develop flavor; remove from heat. Stir in vinegar, sugar, and salt; stir into drained beans in large bowl; let stand about 30 minutes to season.

2 Stir in green pepper, onion, olives, catsup, and mayonnaise or salad dressing; toss lightly to mix.

3 Shred lettuce coarsely, saving some leafy tops for garnish; place in a large salad bowl. Spoon bean mixture on top; tuck leafy tops around edge.

4 Quarter cheese slices; arrange, overlapping, in 2 circles on top of bean mixture.

67

Red Rice
Makes 6 to 8 servings

  1 large onion, chopped (1 cup)
  1 clove of garlic, minced
  2 tablespoons butter or margarine
  2 tablespoons olive oil
1¼ cups uncooked regular rice
  1 can (1 pound) tomatoes
  1 can (13 ounces) chicken broth
  ½ teaspoon salt
  ½ teaspoon pepper

1 Sauté onion and garlic in butter or margarine and olive oil until soft in a medium-size saucepan.
2 Stir in rice, tomatoes, chicken broth, salt, and pepper; heat to boiling; cover.
3 Cook slowly 15 minutes, or until rice is tender and liquid is absorbed.
4 Fluff up rice with a fork; spoon into a serving bowl. Garnish with several green chili peppers, if you wish.

Guacamole Salad
Makes 6 to 8 servings

  3 or 4 medium-size tomatoes
  2 large firm ripe avocados
  1 small onion, chopped (¼ cup)
  1 green chili pepper, chopped fine
  ½ clove of garlic, minced
  3 tablespoons mayonnaise or salad dressing
  3 tablespoons lemon juice
  1 teaspoon Worcestershire sauce
  ¼ teaspoon salt
    Dash of ground coriander
    Dash of cayenne
    Iceberg lettuce, shredded

1 Halve tomatoes crosswise; scoop out insides into a small bowl; dice. Turn tomatoes upside down on paper toweling to drain.
2 Halve avocados; peel and pit. Mash fruit with a fork in a medium-size bowl.
3 Stir in diced tomato and remaining ingredients, except lettuce. Spoon into tomato shells.
4 Arrange tomatoes on a lettuce-lined platter. Garnish each with several slices of pitted ripe olive and serve with corn chips, if you wish.

Chuckwagon Pecan Bread
Bake at 325° for 1 hour and 20 minutes. Makes one 8x4x2-inch loaf

  3 cups sifted all-purpose flour
  1 cup sugar
  4 teaspoons baking powder

A super, Southwestern bread — Chuckwagon Pecan Bread.

  1 teaspoon salt
  1 cup very finely chopped pecans
  2 teaspoons grated lemon rind
  2 eggs
  1 cup milk
  ¼ cup vegetable oil
    Pecan halves

1 Grease an 8x4x2-inch loaf pan.
2 Sift flour, sugar, baking powder, and salt into a large bowl; stir in chopped pecans and lemon rind.
3 Beat eggs well with milk in a small bowl; stir in oil. Add all at once to flour mixture; stir just until evenly moist. Turn into prepared pan; spread top even. Press pecan halves down center of batter to decorate.
4 Bake in slow oven (325°) 1 hour and 20 minutes, or until a wooden pick inserted in center comes out clean. Cool in pan on a wire rack 10 minutes. Loosen around edges with a knife; turn out onto rack. Place right side up. Cool completely.
5 Wrap loaf in waxed paper, foil, or transparent wrap. Store overnight to mellow flavors and make slicing easier. Cut into thin slices.

Taos Bread
This Pueblo Indian bread is shaped in the form of the sun to honor the Sun God.
Bake at 350.° for 50 minutes. Makes three 13-ounce loaves.

1½ cups water
  3 tablespoons butter or margarine
  1 tablespoon sugar
  3 teaspoons salt
  2 envelopes active dry yeast
  ½ cup very warm water
6½ cups sifted all-purpose flour

1 Combine water, butter or margarine, sugar and salt in a small saucepan. Heat slowly until butter or margarine melts; cool to lukewarm.

2 Sprinkle yeast into very warm water in a large bowl. (Very warm water should feel comfortably warm when dropped on wrist.) Stir until yeast dissolves, then stir in butter mixture.
3 Beat in 4 cups of flour until smooth. Beat in enough remaining flour to make a soft dough.
4 Turn out onto a lightly floured pastry board; knead until smooth and elastic, about 5 minutes, using only as much flour as needed to keep dough from sticking.
5 Place in a greased large bowl; turn to coat all over with shortening; cover with a clean towel. Let rise in a warm place, away from draft, 1½ hours, or until double in bulk.
6 Punch dough down; turn out onto board; knead a few times; divide dough into 3 equal pieces. Shape each piece into a ball. Cover with a towel, let rest 10 minutes.
7 On the pastry board, roll each ball into a 9-inch circle. Fold each circle almost in half. Top circular edge should be about 1 inch from bottom circular edge. Place on greased cooky sheet. With kitchen scissors, make about 6 gashes in the dough, cutting from the circular edge about ⅔ the way inward to the folded edge. Spread the fingers of dough apart so they will not touch each other while baking. Do the same with the remaining 2 balls of dough. Let rise again in warm place, away from draft, 1 hour, or until double in bulk.
8 Bake in moderate oven (350°) 50 minutes, or until breads are golden, and give a hollow sound when tapped. Remove from cooky sheet to wire racks; cool completely.

Fry Bread
Sometimes called sopaipillas. As they cook, they puff blistery golden. Serve them hot as the bread of the meal
Makes 32 pieces

2 cups sifted all-purpose flour
2 teaspoons baking powder
1 teaspoon salt
1 egg
3 tablespoons vegetable oil
½ cup water
  Shortening or vegetable oil for frying

1 Sift flour, baking powder, and salt into a medium-size bowl.
2 Beat egg in a small bowl; stir in vegetable oil and water. Pour over dry ingredients, stirring with a fork until well-blended.
3 Turn out onto a lightly floured pastry cloth or board; knead until smooth; divide dough in half. Roll out each to a 12-inch square, then cut into 16 three-inch squares.
4 Melt enough shortening or pour in enough vegetable oil to make a 2-inch depth in an electric deep-fat fryer or deep heavy saucepan; heat to 380°.
5 Fry squares, 2 or 3 at a time and turning often, 3 to 4 minutes, or until puffed and golden. Lift out with a slotted spoon; drain on paper toweling; keep warm.

THE WEST

Herbed Spitted Chicken
Fresh herbs are a feature of California cooking.
Makes 4 servings

3 tablespoons minced fresh rosemary
  OR: 2 tablespoons leaf rosemary, crumbled
3 tablespoons minced fresh tarragon

What more appropriate from the Golden West than golden roasting chickens, spitted to juicy perfection and delicately scented with rosemary?

OR: 2 tablespoons leaf tarragon, crumbled
Dry white wine or chicken broth
½ cup (1 stick) butter or margarine
1 teaspoon salt
¼ teaspoon freshly ground pepper
1 roasting chicken, weighing about 3½ to 4
   pounds

1 Combine fresh rosemary and tarragon in a small bowl. If you are using dried herbs, combine with ⅓ cup dry white wine or broth in a small bowl. Let stand 1 hour. Strain; reserve liquid. Add butter or margarine to the herbs; blend well.
2 Sprinkle the cavity of the chicken with part of the salt and pepper and put in about 1 tablespoon herb butter. Carefully loosen the skin over the breast with your fingers and press in about 1 to 2 tablespoons of the herb butter. Truss the bird, balance it on the spit and fasten it securely.
3 Melt the remaining herb butter and brush over bird. Sprinkle it with remaining salt and pepper. Combine the remaining herb butter with an equal quantity of wine or broth, or, if using dried herbs, with reserved wine or broth.
4 Roast the chicken for about 2½ hours, basting it frequently with the butter-wine mixture. If possible, put a pan under the bird to catch the juices. Skim off the fat and pour a little juice over each piece of carved chicken.

Grilled Lemon Chicken
Makes 4 to 6 servings

½ cup lemon juice
½ cup (1 stick) butter or margarine, melted
1 teaspoon leaf thyme, crumbled
   OR: 1 tablespoon minced fresh thyme
¼ teaspoon liquid red pepper seasoning
2 broiler-fryers (about 2½ pounds each), quartered
   Salt
   Freshly ground pepper

1 Combine lemon juice, butter or margarine, thyme and pepper seasoning in a small bowl.
2 Sprinkle the chickens with salt and pepper. Place the chickens, bone side down, on the grill over hot coals. Brush with the basting sauce.
3 Grill for 40 minutes, turning over once. Baste frequently with the sauce. Serve with the remaining basting sauce poured over the chickens.
Note: Adjust the heat if chicken is cooking too fast.

Lemon Relish
For meats and poultry.
Makes about 1½ cups

2 large lemons
6 green onions, with green tops
½ green pepper, seeded
¼ cup parsley sprigs
1 cup chopped celery
½ teaspoon dry mustard
¼ teaspoon ground cardamom
1 teaspoon salt
1 small hot red pepper, seeded and chopped
   OR: ½ teaspoon liquid red pepper seasoning
1 tablespoon sugar

1 Grate lemons and reserve the grated peel. Cut off all the remaining yellow and white peel of lemons.
2 Put lemons, green onions, pepper, parsley, and celery through the coarse blade of a meat grinder, or whirl coarsely in a blender. Stir in reserved, grated lemon rind.
3 Add mustard, cardamom, salt, chopped pepper, or red pepper seasoning and sugar. Refrigerate, covered, overnight to ripen.

Crab Meat Louis
Makes 8 servings

⅓ cup cream for whipping
1 cup mayonnaise or salad dressing
¼ cup chili sauce
2 tablespoons minced onion
2 tablespoons minced parsley
2 pounds (about 4 cups) cooked, picked-over, flaked crab meat
4 large ripe avocados, halved
   Lettuce

1 Beat cream until stiff in a large bowl.
2 Add mayonnaise or salad dressing, chili sauce, onion, and parsley; blend well. Add crab meat; toss. Serve in avocado halves with crisp lettuce.

Cioppino
A San Francisco specialty.
Makes 8 servings

1 large onion, chopped (1 cup)
1 medium-size green pepper, halved, seeded, and chopped
½ cup sliced celery
1 carrot, pared and shredded
3 cloves of garlic, minced
3 tablespoons olive oil
2 cans (1 pound each) tomatoes

From San Francisco's waterfront comes this California classic—Cioppino, a robust, seafood-rich spoon soup.

1 can (8 ounces) tomato sauce
1 teaspoon leaf basil, crumbled
1 bay leaf
1 teaspoon salt
¼ teaspoon pepper
1 pound fresh or frozen halibut steak
1 dozen mussels or 1 dozen clams in shell (see note)
1½ cups dry white wine
1 package (8 ounces) frozen, shelled, de-veined shrimp
½ pound fresh or frozen scallops
2 tablespoons minced parsley

1 Sauté onion, green pepper, celery, carrot and garlic in olive oil until soft in a kettle or Dutch oven.

2 Stir in tomatoes, tomato sauce, basil, bay leaf, salt and pepper; heat to boiling; reduce heat; cover; simmer 2 hours. Discard bay leaf.

3 While sauce simmers, remove the skin from the halibut; cut into serving-size pieces. Using a stiff brush, thoroughly scrub the mussels, cutting off their "beards," or the clams, under running water to remove any residue of mud and sand.

4 Stir wine into sauce in kettle. Add halibut, shrimp and scallops. Simmer, covered, 10 minutes longer.

5 Place mussels or clams in a layer on top of fish in kettle; cover; steam 5 to 10 minutes, or until the shells are fully opened and fish flakes easily. (Discard any unopened mussels or clams.)

6 Ladle into soup plates or bowls. Sprinkle with parsley. Serve with sourdough bread, or crusty French or Italian bread.

Note: 1 can (10 ounces) clams in shell may be substituted for fresh clams.

Oriental Skewered Shrimp
A fine entrée from the hibachi.
Makes 4 servings

¾ cup medium dry California sherry
¼ cup soy sauce
1 teaspoon sugar
½ teaspoon ground ginger
36 raw medium-size shrimp, shelled (about 1¼ pounds)
  Wooden or bamboo skewers, about 9 inches long
  Cherry tomatoes
  Yellow pickled peppers

1 Combine sherry, soy sauce, sugar and ginger in a small saucepan. Heat just to boiling; remove from heat; cool to room temperature.

2 Wash shrimp. Thread 3 shrimp lengthwise, through the center, heads doubled up against the tails, on each skewer. Thread a cherry tomato or yellow pickled pepper at end of each skewer. Place on a platter and brush with sauce on all sides. Refrigerate for 1 hour.

3 Grill over medium coals for 6 to 10 minutes, turning once and brushing frequently with the sauce, until nicely glazed. Serve piping hot.

Wyoming Basque Potatoes
Makes 8 servings

1 medium-size onion, chopped (½ cup)
1 small clove of garlic, crushed
2 tablespoons olive oil
¾ cup chopped parsley
¼ cup chopped pimiento
1 teaspoon salt
⅛ teaspoon pepper
1 envelope instant chicken broth or 1 teaspoon granulated chicken bouillon
1 cup water
6 medium-size potatoes (about 3 pounds)

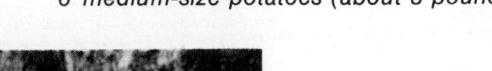

Because California can boast "outdoor weather" almost 365 days each year, eating alfresco is very nearly an every-day occurrence. An outdoor favorite—zippy Oriental Skewered Shrimp.

Wyoming Basque Potatoes, a favorite shepherd dish.

1 Sauté onion and garlic in olive oil until soft in a medium-size skillet; stir in parsley, pimiento, salt, pepper, chicken broth, and water. Remove from heat; reserve.
2 Pare potatoes and thinly slice (you should have about 6 cups). Layer potato slices in the broth in the skillet; heat to boiling; reduce heat; cover. Simmer about 20 minutes, or until tender.
3 Remove potatoes with a slotted spoon to a heated serving dish. Spoon remaining cooking liquid over potatoes.

Barbecued Corn

Foil-wrap technique works indoors or out; gives real barbecue taste to fresh corn.
Bake at 400° for 25 minutes. Makes 6 servings

6 ears of corn
½ cup (1 stick) butter or margarine
3 tablespoons bottled barbecue sauce
½ teaspoon salt
¼ teaspoon pepper

1 Husk corn and remove silk. Place each ear on a double-thick sheet of foil.
2 Melt butter or margarine in a small saucepan; stir in barbecue sauce, salt, and pepper; brush over corn. Wrap foil around ears; twist ends to seal. Place in a large shallow pan.
3 Bake in hot oven (400°), turning often, 25 minutes. Serve from foil wrappers. To cook corn outdoors, place foil-wrapped ears on grill over hot coals. Grill, turning often, 15 to 25 minutes, depending on temperature of coals.

Cucumber Salad

Makes 4 to 6 servings

3 large cucumbers
⅓ cup vinegar
2 tablespoons water
¼ cup sugar
1 teaspoon salt
¼ teaspoon freshly ground pepper
1 tablespoon minced dill

1 Peel the cucumbers; slice wafer thin. Put slices into a bowl of water and ice cubes. Refrigerate for 1 hour; drain; pat dry with paper toweling. Arrange in serving bowl.
2 Combine vinegar, water, sugar, salt and pepper in a 1-cup measure. Pour mixture over cucumbers. Refrigerate for at least 1 hour. At serving time, drain off liquid; sprinkle with dill.

Honolulu Chicken Salad

Chicken and vegetables marinated in a soy-seasoned dressing.
Makes 6 servings

1 stewing chicken (about 5 pounds), not cut up
3½ cups water
1 medium-size onion, sliced
Handful of celery tops
2 teaspoons salt
¼ teaspoon oregano
1 bay leaf
Ginger-soy Dressing (recipe follows)
1 package (10 ounces) frozen peas
1 package (9 ounces) frozen artichoke hearts
1 large head of lettuce (Boston, leaf, or iceberg)
Pine nuts or shredded blanched almonds
1 pimiento, diced
1 cup thinly sliced celery
1 small green pepper, cut in thin strips
1 can (about 13 ounces) frozen pineapple chunks, thawed and drained
Shredded coconut

1 Place chicken in large kettle; add water, onion, celery tops, salt, oregano, and bay leaf. Cover; heat to boiling, then simmer 1½ to 2 hours, or until chicken is tender. Take chicken from broth and let drain in shallow pan until cool enough to handle. (Strain broth and save to make soup.)
2 Remove skin from chicken, then pull away dark and white meat in large pieces from frame (this is easy to do while it is still warm; save any little bits and pieces to add to soup).
3 Cut chicken into bite-size pieces; place in a shallow pan; pour ¼ cup *Ginger-Soy Dressing* over. Cover and chill.
4 Cook peas and artichoke hearts in separate small saucepans, following label directions; drain. Place each in small bowl and stir into each 2 tablespoons *Ginger-Soy Dressing;* cover; chill.
5 When ready to put salad together, arrange lettuce leaves in bottom and around sides of large salad bowl; top with mounds of marinated chicken, peas sprinkled with nuts, and artichokes garnished with pimiento. Fill in spaces

73

with sliced celery, green-pepper strips, and pineapple chunks sprinkled with coconut. Serve with remaining dressing.

GINGER-SOY DRESSING—Combine ½ cup vegetable oil, ¼ cup lemon juice, 2 tablespoons pineapple syrup (drained from pineapple chunks), 1 tablespoon soy sauce, ½ teaspoon salt, and ½ teaspoon ground ginger in 2-cup jar with tight-fitting cover. Shake well. Makes about 1 cup.

Caesar Salad

This nationally famous California salad is often used as a first course.

Makes 6 to 8 servings

2 cloves of garlic
¾ cup olive oil
2 cups bread cubes (4 slices)
2 large or 3 small heads romaine lettuce
½ teaspoon freshly ground pepper
½ teaspoon salt
2 medium eggs, soft-cooked for 1 minute
3 tablespoons lemon juice
6 anchovy fillets, drained and cut into small pieces (optional)
½ cup freshly grated Parmesan cheese

1 Cut one of the garlic cloves in half; rub cut surface over inside of a large salad bowl. Discard. Brown remaining garlic clove in ¼ cup of the olive oil in a large skillet. Remove browned garlic clove; add bread cubes; brown on all sides. Drain croutons on paper toweling.
2 Break romaine leaves into bite-size pieces into salad bowl. Sprinkle with pepper and salt. Add remaining olive oil. Mix gently until every piece of lettuce is glistening with oil. Break eggs into the middle of the romaine and pour lemon juice directly over the eggs. Toss gently but thoroughly until there is a creamy look to the salad. Add the anchovies and cheese; taste, adding more salt, pepper and lemon juice, if desired. Go easy on the salt since the Parmesan is salty; toss. Add the croutons and toss again; serve immediately so that the croutons remain crisp.

74

Plentiful Fruit Platter

Appetizer of the West's natural bounty, arranged around cream-mint dressing.

Makes 8 servings

1 small head romaine
1 small honeydew melon

1 small cantaloupe
1 pint strawberries
2 small seedless oranges
2 small avocados
2 tablespoons lemon juice
½ pound red grapes
½ pound seedless green grapes
Mint-cream Dressing (recipe follows)

1 Separate romaine leaves; wash and dry well.
2 Halve honeydew melon; scoop out seeds; cut into balls with a melonball cutter or the ½ teaspoon of a measuring-spoon set. Quarter cantaloupe; scoop out seeds; pare. Wash strawberries, hull, and halve. Pare oranges; cut into thick slices. Halve avocados and pit; brush cut surfaces with lemon juice to keep color bright.
3 To arrange platter, set aside several small romaine leaves, then place remainder at one end of a large deep platter or shallow bowl; stand avocado halves in front of romaine. Set dressing bowl next to avocados to hold them in place.
4 Arrange cantaloupe quarters, spoke-fashion, around front of bowl; fill in sections between with strawberries and honeydew balls. Tuck red grapes into avocado hollows, orange slices behind avocados, and green grapes at sides. Spoon Mint-Cream Dressing into bowl; garnish with saved small romaine leaves. To serve, let guests take their choice of fruits and help themselves to dressing.

MINT-CREAM DRESSING—In a small bowl, blend 1 cup dairy sour cream, 3 tablespoons chopped fresh mint, 2 tablespoons 10X (confectioners' powdered) sugar , and ¼ teaspoon ground cardamom; cover. Chill at least 30 minutes. Makes about 1 cup.

Avocado Salad Bowl
Makes 8 servings

8 cups broken mixed salad greens
1 large firm ripe avocado, halved, peeled, pitted, and sliced
⅓ cup vegetable oil
2 tablespoons cider vinegar
1 tablespoon honey
½ teaspoon sugar
¼ teaspoon salt
Dash of paprika

1 Place greens in a large salad bowl; arrange avocado slices in a pretty pattern on top.
2 Combine remaining ingredients in a jar with a tight lid; shake well to mix. Drizzle over salad; toss lightly until the greens are evenly coated with dressing.

THE WEST

Californians dote on Plentiful Fruit Platter which can double as dessert or salad. Small wonder because the recipe makes the most of California's vast cornucopia of versatile fruits.

Caesar Salad, that great California creation, may not be Californian at all. Some say the recipe was actually developed in Tijuana, Mexico, then quickly whisked across the border by appreciative California chefs.

Western Salad Bowl
Makes 6 servings

½ medium-size head iceberg lettuce, shredded
  (about 4 cups)
1 small red apple, halved, cored, and sliced
  thin
½ small Bermuda onion, peeled and sliced thin
½ cup thinly sliced celery
½ cup bottled sweet-garlic French dressing

1 Combine lettuce, apple, onion, and celery in
a large salad bowl.
2 Drizzle dressing over top; toss lightly to mix.

Golden Gate Salad Bowl
Makes 8 servings

1 head Boston lettuce
2 bunches watercress
1 small ripe avocado
¼ cup lemon juice
2 tablespoons water
⅔ cup vegetable oil
½ teaspoon salt
½ teaspoon sugar
3 medium-size oranges, pared and sectioned
3 preserved kumquats, sliced
⅓ cup chopped pecans

1 Trim lettuce; wash; drain. Wash watercress;
snip sprigs apart, discarding heavy stems. Wrap
lettuce and watercress in towels to absorb
moisture. Chill several hours till crisp.
2 Halve avocado, peel, pit, and dice. Combine
with lemon juice, water, oil, salt, and sugar in
an electric-blender container; cover. Whirl until
smooth. (If you do not have a blender, mash
avocado in a bowl, with a fork, then add other
ingredients; beat until smooth.) Chill.
3 Line a large salad bowl with lettuce leaves;
break remainder into bite-size pieces in bowl.
Add watercress.
4 Tuck orange sections and kumquat slices
among leaves; sprinkle pecans over all. Pass
avocado dressing separately.

North Beach Tossed Salad
Makes 6 servings

1 medium-size head Boston lettuce
1 medium-size head romaine lettuce

2 large ripe tomatoes, peeled and cut into
  bite-size wedges
1 onion, thinly sliced
2 garlic cloves, minced
2 tablespoons minced chives
1 tablespoon chopped fresh basil or, 2 teaspoons leaf basil, crumbled
12 large pitted green olives
12 large pitted ripe olives
1 teaspoon prepared hot mustard
2 tablespoons red wine vinegar
6 tablespoons olive oil
  Salt
  Freshly ground pepper
6 large red radishes, thinly sliced

1 Prepare the salad greens 2 to 4 hours ahead
of time. Wash and core the lettuce, and tear
the leaves into bite-size pieces. Wrap the lettuce
in paper toweling. Put it in the refrigerator to
dry and crisp.
2 Wash greens; break into bite-size pieces in
a salad bowl; cover; chill.
3 Add tomatoes, onion, garlic, chives, basil and
olives.
4 Stir the mustard into the vinegar and sprinkle
over the salad; toss. Sprinkle with the oil and
salt and pepper; toss again. Sprinkle the radish
slices over the top.

San Joaquin Fruit Salad
Surprise salad plays onion and buttermilk
against two flavors of citrus.
Makes 6 servings

1 medium-size head iceberg lettuce, shredded
  (6 cups)
1 seedless grapefruit, pared and sectioned
2 seedless oranges, pared and sectioned
  OR: 1 can (1 pound) orange and grapefruit
  sections
½ medium-size Bermuda onion, diced (1½
  cups)
½ cup buttermilk
1 tablespoon lemon juice
2 tablespoons vegetable oil
1 tablespoon sugar
½ teaspoon salt

1 Place lettuce in a large salad bowl; arrange
fruit sections in a circle on top; spoon onion
in center. (If using canned fruit sections, drain
first, saving syrup for fruit punch.)

*More of the West Coast's handsome harvest of fruits
and vegetables, served up as fresh, "unfussed-over"
salads—the favorites from Seattle to San Diego.*

76

2 Combine buttermilk, lemon juice, vegetable oil, sugar, and salt in a jar with a tight-fitting lid; shake well to mix.
3 Just before serving, drizzle over salad; toss lightly to mix.

California Salad Bowl
A lavish fruit-and-vegetable bowl from the state that does salads in a big way.
Makes 6 to 8 servings

3 jars (6 ounces each) marinated artichoke hearts
1 medium-size head iceberg lettuce, broken into bite-size pieces
3 tomatoes, cut into wedges
½ medium-size cantaloupe, pared and diced
¼ cup mayonnaise or salad dressing
¼ cup lemon juice
1 teaspoon seasoned salt
1 teaspoon sugar

1 Drain liquid from artichokes into a small bowl.
2 Place lettuce in a large salad bowl. Arrange artichoke hearts, tomatoes, and cantaloupe on top.
3 Beat mayonnaise or salad dressing, lemon juice, seasoned salt, and sugar into artichoke liquid.
4 Just before serving, drizzle over salad; toss lightly to mix.

Cumin Tortillas
Makes 24 tortillas

¾ cup (1½ sticks) butter or margarine, softened
1 teaspoon ground cumin or cardamom
2 dozen canned tortillas

1 Blend the butter or margarine and ground cumin or cardamom in a small bowl. Spread each tortilla lightly on one side with a little of the mixture. Make 2 stacks with 1 dozen tortillas each, buttered side up. Wrap each stack separately in foil.
2 Heat on a corner of the grill for about 12 minutes, or for 20 minutes in a slow oven (300°). Keep one stack warm while you serve the first. Each guest rolls or folds his own, or you may do this for your guests.

Klondike Pancakes
Makes about 16 four-inch pancakes

1 cup milk
¼ cup shortening
2 tablespoons sugar
1 teaspoon salt
1 envelope active dry yeast
¼ cup very warm water
1 egg
1 cup sifted all-purpose flour

1 Scald milk with shortening in medium-size saucepan; stir in sugar and salt; cool to lukewarm.
2 Sprinkle yeast into very warm water in medium-size bowl. (Warm water should feel comfortably warm when dropped on wrist.) Stir until yeast dissolves, then stir in cooled milk mixture; beat in egg and flour. Cover; let rise in warm place, away from draft, 1 hour, or until double in bulk.
3 When ready to bake, heat griddle slowly. Test temperature by sprinkling on a few drops of water; when drops bounce about, temperature is right. (If using electric griddle, follow manufacturer's directions for heating.) Grease lightly with butter, margarine, or salad oil, then repeat greasing before each baking.
4 Stir batter down; ladle, a scant ¼ cup for each cake, onto griddle. Bake 1 to 2 minutes, or until bubbles appear on top; turn; bake 1 to 2 minutes longer. Stir batter before baking each batch. Serve hot with butter or margarine and syrup.

California Fruit Soup
Californians of Scandinavian descent, such as the Danes of Solvang, eat these typical California fruits as a first course soup. Others will enjoy them as a splendidly refreshing dessert.
Makes 4 servings

1 cup dried apricots (from an 8-ounce package)
1 cup pitted dried prunes (from 15-ounce package)
5 cups water
1 can (6 ounces) frozen orange juice concentrate
1 lemon
1 three-inch piece stick cinnamon
2 tablespoons quick-cooking tapioca
½ cup sugar
½ cup dairy sour cream
¼ cup shredded orange rind

1 Combine apricots, prunes, water and orange juice concentrate in a large saucepan. Let stand for 30 minutes.

Monterey Crêpes, thin pancakes filled with sliced strawberries and peaches, are a fitting finish for a fine meal.

2 Pare the thin bright yellow rind from the lemon with a vegetable parer. Add with cinnamon, tapioca and sugar to the fruits.
3 Simmer, covered, for about 10 minutes, or until almost tender. Fruits should not be mushy. Taste the soup; if desired, stir in 1 tablespoon lemon juice or more for a stronger lemon flavor. Remove cinnamon stick and lemon peel. Cool.
4 Serve in glass serving dish or individual bowls with a garnish of sour cream and orange rind.

Sponge Cake with Oranges
A luscious way to dress up California oranges —slip juicy sections between golden sponge cakes, then crown with a fluffy cloud of whipped cream.
Makes one 9-inch, 2-layer cake

 3 navel oranges
½ cup cream for whipping
 2 tablespoons sugar
¼ teaspoon ground ginger (optional)
 2 freshly-baked 9-inch sponge cake layers

1 Pare oranges with a sharp knife, removing every trace of yellow and white skin. Section oranges into a small bowl, removing any seeds.
2 Just before serving, whip cream until stiff in a small bowl.
3 Arrange half the orange sections on one of

the cake layers. Combine sugar and ginger in a cup; sprinkle over oranges. Top with remaining layer.
4 Arrange remaining orange sections on top Spoon whipped cream over.

Monterey Crêpes
The West takes advantage of its bountiful fruits for these showy treats.
Makes 4 servings

 2 pints strawberries
 6 medium-size peaches
 1 tablespoon lemon juice
½ cup sugar (for fruit)
½ teaspoon ground cinnamon
 3 eggs
 2 tablespoons vegetable oil
 1 cup milk
⅔ cup sifted all-purpose flour
 1 tablespoon sugar (for crêpes)
¼ teaspoon salt
¼ teaspoon mace
   Butter or margarine
 1 cup dairy sour cream

1 Wash strawberries, hull, and slice into a medium-size bowl. Peel peaches, halve, pit, and slice; combine with strawberries. Sprinkle with

79

lemon juice, the ½ cup sugar, and cinnamon; let stand while making crêpes.

2 Beat eggs slightly in a medium-size bowl; beat in vegetable oil and milk. Add flour, the 1 tablespoon sugar, salt, and mace; beat 3 minutes longer. (Batter will be thin.)

3 Heat a 7-inch frying pan slowly; test temperature by sprinkling in a few drops of water; when drops bounce about, temperature is right. Grease lightly with butter or margarine. Measure batter, ¼ cup at a time, into pan, tilting pan to cover bottom completely.

4 Bake 1 to 2 minutes, or until top appears dry and underside is golden; turn. Bake 1 to 2 minutes longer, or until bottom browns. Repeat with remaining batter, lightly buttering pan before each baking, to make 8 crêpes.

5 As each crêpe is baked, spoon about 4 tablespoons of the fruit mixture on top, setting aside 3 or 4 peach slices for garnish, if you wish. Roll up crêpes, jelly-roll fashion. Place in a shallow serving dish. When ready to serve, spoon sour cream in a ribbon over crêpes. Garnish with mint sprigs, if you wish. Serve warm.

●

Alaska Mint Pie

Bake at 325° for 10 minutes, then at 450° for 4 minutes. Makes 8 servings

    1 package (5 ounces) shortbread cookies, crushed (about 1⅓ cups)
    ½ cup finely chopped pecans
    ⅓ cup firmly packed light brown sugar
    6 tablespoons (¾ stick) butter or margarine, melted
    ½ cup water
    10 tablespoons granulated sugar
    2 tablespoons green crème de menthe
    1 quart vanilla ice cream, softened
    ½ cup cream for whipping
      Few drops green food coloring
    3 egg whites
    ⅛ teaspoon cream of tartar

1 Blend shortbread crumbs, pecans, brown sugar, and butter or margarine in a medium-size bowl. Press mixture firmly over bottom and side of a 9-inch pie plate.

2 Bake in slow oven (325°) 10 minutes, or until set. Cool completely on a wire rack.

3 Combine water with 4 tablespoons of the sugar in a small saucepan; cover. Bring to boiling; uncover; continue boiling, without stirring, 7 minutes. Remove from heat; cool slightly; stir in crème de menthe; cool completely.

4 Spread half the ice cream in an even layer in cooled pie shell; cover; freeze until firm.

5 Combine cream with food coloring in a small bowl; beat until stiff. Fold in 2 tablespoons of

the cooled crème de menthe syrup into the cream. Spread evenly over firm ice cream in pie shell. Freeze until firm. Top with remaining ice cream. Freeze until firm. Pie may be wrapped in foil or plastic wrap, and kept frozen for a week before the buffet.

6 Beat egg whites with cream of tartar until foamy-white and double in volume in a medium-size bowl. Beat in the remaining 6 tablespoons sugar, 1 tablespoon at a time, until meringue stands in firm peaks. Pile meringue onto filling, sealing firmly to crust edge and swirling into peaks. Freeze overnight.

7 Just before serving, brown meringue until lightly golden in very hot oven (450°) for 4 minutes. Drizzle with remaining crème de menthe syrup; serve at once.

●

Grape Harvest Pie

Juicy fruit, fragrant spice, and nippy lemon blend pleasingly in this fall dessert .

Bake at 400° for 50 minutes. Makes 1 nine-inch pie

    1 package piecrust mix
    2 pounds Emperor grapes, washed, halved, and seeded (about 5½ cups)
    1 cup sugar
    ⅓ cup flour
    ½ teaspoon salt
    ½ teaspoon mace
    2 eggs, slightly beaten
    ½ teaspoon grated lemon rind
    2 tablespoons lemon juice
    2 tablespoons butter or margarine

1 Prepare piecrust mix, following label directions, or make pastry from your own favorite 2-crust recipe. Roll out half to a 12-inch round on lightly floured pastry cloth or board; fit into a 9-inch pie plate; trim overhang to ½ inch.

2 Combine grapes, sugar, flour, salt, and mace in medium-size bowl; stir in eggs, lemon rind, and lemon juice. Pour into prepared pastry shell; dot with butter or margarine.

3 Roll out remaining pastry to an 11-inch round; cut several slits near center to allow steam to escape; cover pie; trim overhang to ½ inch; turn edges under and press together to seal; flute.

4 Bake in hot oven (400°) 50 minutes, or until top is golden-brown and juices bubble up. Cool on wire rack about an hour; serve warm.

●

Macadamia Nut Pie

Bake at 325° for 1 hour and 10 minutes. Makes 1 nine-inch pie

80

½ package piecrust mix
4 eggs
⅔ cup sugar
¾ cup light corn syrup
¼ cup honey
3 tablespoons butter or margarine, melted
    and cooled
½ teaspoon vanilla
1¼ cups chopped macadamia nuts

1 Prepare piecrust mix, following label directions, or make pastry from your favorite single-crust recipe. Roll out to a 12-inch round on a lightly floured pastry cloth or board; fit into a 9-inch pie plate. Trim overhang to ½ inch; turn under, flush with rim; flute to make a stand-up edge.
2 Combine eggs, sugar, corn syrup, honey, butter or margarine, and vanilla in large bowl of electric mixer; beat about 5 minutes at medium speed, or until light-colored and frothy. Stir in nuts.
3 Pour nut mixture into prepared pastry shell.
4 Bake in slow oven (325°) 1 hour and 10 minutes, or until crust is golden and filling is set at edges but still slightly soft in center. (Do not overbake.) Cool completely on a wire rack. Garnish with whipped cream and additional chopped macadamia nuts, if you wish.

Cheese Cake Hawaiian
Bake at 350° for 10 minutes. Makes 12 servings

1 cup vanilla wafer crumbs
2 tablespoons sugar (for crust)
2 tablespoons melted butter or margarine
1 package (6 ounces) lemon-flavor gelatin
1 cup boiling water
3 eggs, separated
1 container (1 pound) cream-style cottage
    cheese
2 teaspoons vanilla
¼ teaspoon ground cardamom
½ cup sugar (for filling)
    Hawaiian Topping (recipe follows)

1 Combine crumbs with the 2 tablespoons sugar in a medium-size bowl; blend in melted butter or margarine. Press evenly over bottom and side of a buttered 8-inch spring-form pan.
2 Bake in moderate oven (350°) 10 minutes, or until crumbs are set. Cool while making filling.
3 Dissolve gelatin in boiling water in a medium-size saucepan. Beat egg yolks slightly in a small bowl. Slowly stir half of hot gelatin mixture into beaten eggs; stir back into pan. Cook until mixture thickens slightly.
4 Sieve cottage cheese into a large bowl; blend in gelatin mixture, vanilla, and cardamom. Chill until thickened.
5 Beat egg whites until foamy-white and double in volume in a small bowl. Beat in the ½ cup sugar, 1 tablespoon at a time, until meringue stands in firm peaks. Fold into cottage cheese mixture. Pour into prepared crumb crust. Chill 4 hours, or until firm.
6 Loosen cake around edge with a knife; release spring and carefully lift off side of pan. Slide cake, still on metal base, onto a serving plate. Top with *Hawaiian Topping**. Chill 1 hour, or until serving time.
   HAWAIIAN TOPPING—Drain the syrup from 1 eight-ounce can sliced pineapple into a small saucepan; blend in 2 teaspoons cornstarch. Cook, stirring constantly, until mixture thickens and bubbles 3 minutes. Stir in 2 tablespoons syrup from maraschino cherries; cool slightly. Arrange pineapple slices and 4 maraschino cherries on top of cheese cake. Brush glaze over fruits and cheese cake.

Apricot Creams
Dried fruits make the nicest bite-size sweets—like little no-cook candies.

Makes about 5 dozen

½ cup golden raisins
½ cup toasted slivered almonds
1 cup 10X (confectioners' powdered) sugar
2 tablespoons dairy sour cream
1 package (11 ounces) dried apricot halves

1 Chop raisins and almonds; blend with 10X sugar and sour cream in a small bowl.
2 Separate apricot halves; spoon a scant teaspoonful raisin mixture in center of each half. Chill.

APPETIZERS and HORS D´OEUVRES

APPETIZERS AND HORS D´OEUVRES: DIPS, DUNKS AND SPREADS, NIBBLES, CANAPÉS AND HORS D´OEUVRES

Good beginners, the appetizers and hors d´oeuvres included here. Good party starters. Some are a snap to make, others frankly intricate (but well worth the time and trouble).

Any rules for serving? A few. Light appetizers should precede the hearty dinner, heavier ones the not-so-filling meal (these are also the most appropriate for cocktail parties). All appetizers and hors d´oeuvres should be sharp or tart to hone the appetite.

Dips are for dipping, not dripping, so they should be fairly thick (the same goes for spreads). Canapés (mini open-face sandwiches) and hors d´oeuvres (micro finger foods) should be bite-size or at least small enough to down in two bites because guests will be juggling drinks and cigarettes as well as nibbling.

Cold appetizers, generally speaking, are welcome in summer (also before luncheon), hot appetizers in winter. *All* appetizers, whether hot or cold, light or filling, plain or fancy, should look freshly made, never fussed over or *left* over. Appetizer trays should be replenished and tidied often, wilting parsley sprigs replaced with crinkly new ruffs, fading radish roses with crisp red ones.

Very simply, appetizers and hors d´oeuvres should look—*and be*—"good enough to eat."

DIPS, DUNKS AND SPREADS

83

Oahu Dip-And-Chip Tray
Shape the cheese spread into a "mountain" and frame with raw nibbles and corn dippers or favorite chips.
Makes 16 servings

1 ½ pounds cream-style cottage cheese (3 cups)
3 packages (8 ounces each) cream cheese, softened

What better way to get a party off to a fast start? Simply put out dazzling arrays of hot and cold hors d'oeuvres and canapés, loaded with color and flavor.

6 ounces blue cheese, crumbled
1 teaspoon seasoned salt
2 teaspoons Worcestershire sauce
    Few drops liquid red pepper seasoning
¾ cup finely chopped parsley
    Pitted ripe olives
1 cherry tomato
4 large carrots, pared and sliced diagonally
2 large cucumbers, scored and sliced
8 stalks celery, sliced
2 large green peppers, quartered, seeded, and cut in bite-size pieces
1 small head of cauliflower, separated in flowerets
    Flower-shape corn snacks

1 Combine cottage, cream, and blue cheeses, seasoned salt, Worcestershire sauce, and liquid red pepper seasoning in a large bowl; beat until completely blended; cover. Chill several hours, or until firm enough to handle.
2 Spoon cheese mixture in the center of a large serving tray; pat into a "mountain" shape, then press parsley into cheese to cover the bottom two thirds.
3 Cut olives lengthwise into 8 wedges each; arrange over cheese in a spiral pattern almost to top.
4 Slice cherry tomato into eighths from blossom end almost to stem end; separate cuts slightly to form petals; stand on top of cheese. Arrange carrot, cucumber, and celery slices, green pepper pieces, cauliflowerets, and corn snacks in separate piles around cheese.

Garlic Cheese Dip
Makes 2 cups

2 cups (16-ounce carton) dairy sour cream
1 envelope cheese-garlic salad dressing mix
½ teaspoon dried parsley flakes

Combine all ingredients in a small bowl, chill several hours to blend flavors, then serve with crackers or crisp vegetable sticks.

Tomato Dip
Makes 2 cups

1 can (10¾-ounces) condensed tomato soup
1 3-ounce package cream cheese, softened

¼ cup chopped ripe olives
2 tablespoons chopped parsley
⅛ teaspoon pepper

Blend tomato soup and cream cheese in a medium-size bowl until smooth. Stir in remaining ingredients and chill about an hour before serving.

Bean-Onion Dip
Makes 2 cups

1 can (1 pound) pork-and-beans
1 small onion, peeled and quartered
¼ cup molasses
2 tablespoons prepared mustard

Whirl all ingredients in an electric blender until smooth. (If you do not have a blender, press beans through a sieve; grate the onion instead of quartering, then mix all ingredients together). Serve with crisp crackers.

Guacamole
Makes about 2 cups

1 medium-size ripe avocado
½ cup mayonnaise or salad dressing
2 tablespoons lemon juice
1 teaspoon salt
1 teaspoon grated onion
¼ teaspoon liquid red pepper seasoning
1 large tomato, peeled, chopped and drained

1 Halve avocado, peel, pit and mash in a medium-size bowl. Blend in remaining ingredients, cover and chill. (Dip will stay bright green several hours.)
2 When ready to serve, spoon into small bowls and set out plenty of crisp corn sticks.

Sweet-Sour Dip
Makes about 1⅓ cups

4 slices bacon, diced
1 package (8 ounces) cream cheese, softened
¼ cup bottled sweet-sour salad dressing
2 tablespoons milk

1 Sauté bacon until crisp in a small frying pan; remove to paper toweling to drain.
2 Combine cream cheese, salad dressing and milk in a medium-size bowl; beat until smooth. Fold in bacon, chill several hours, then serve with crackers or crisp vegetable sticks.

Everything the well dressed party needs—plenty of crisp chips and an assortment of savory, snappy dips.

Spanish Tuna Dip
Makes about 2 cups

½ cup (1 stick) butter or margarine
1 can (about 7 ounces) water-pack tuna, drained and flaked
4 teaspoons lemon juice
¼ cup mayonnaise or salad dressing
2 tablespoons chopped stuffed green olives

1 Cream butter or margarine until soft in a small bowl; beat in tuna, lemon juice, and mayonnaise or salad dressing; fold in olives. Chill.
2 Spoon into small dip bowls. Serve with crisp carrot and celery sticks or crackers.

Clam-Cream Dip
Your zippy seasoning helper? Versatile horseradish dip mix in an envelope.
Makes 2 cups

1 cup (8-ounce carton) cream-style cottage cheese
1 package (3 or 4 ounces) cream cheese
1 packet (about 1 tablespoon) horseradish dip mix or 2 teaspoons prepared horseradish
1 teaspoon Worcestershire sauce
1 can (about 10 ½ ounces) minced clams, drained
3 to 4 tablespoons light or table cream
Paprika

85

1 Blend cottage cheese, cream cheese, dip mix or horseradish, and Worcestershire sauce in a medium-size bowl; stir in clams. Chill.

2 When ready to serve, beat in cream to thin mixture enough for dipping; spoon into small bowls; sprinkle with paprika. Serve with crisp potato chips, if you wish.

●

Kauai Crab Spread
Makes about 2½ cups

8 ounces (half a 1-pound package) frozen crab meat, thawed and drained
1 cup dairy sour cream
2 teaspoons curry powder
½ teaspoon onion salt
½ teaspoon garlic powder
¼ cup minced chutney
¼ cup flaked coconut

Mix all ingredients and chill well. Serve as a spread for crackers or melba rounds.

●

Tivoli Cheese Mold
Nippy blue and cream cheeses go into this zesty spread.
Makes 6 servings

1 envelope unflavored gelatin
½ cup cold water
½ cup light cream or table cream
1 package (8 ounces) cream cheese
¼ cup crumbled blue cheese

2 tablespoons chopped parsley
½ teaspoon salt
½ teaspoon paprika
½ teaspoon Worcestershire sauce

1 Soften gelatin in water in a small saucepan; heat over low heat, stirring constantly, until gelatin dissolves; remove from heat. Stir in cream.

2 Blend cream cheese with blue cheese in a medium-size bowl; stir in parsley, salt, paprika, and Worcestershire sauce; gradually blend in gelatin-cream mixture. Pour into a 2-cup deep mold. Chill several hours, or until firm.

3 When ready to serve, run a sharp-tip, thin-blade knife around top of mold to loosen, then dip mold *very quickly* in and out of a pan of hot water. Invert onto serving tray. Garnish with a whole strawberry, if you wish.

Sour cream and cream cheese, two great mixers, used here in a garlic dip and red-caviar-bejeweled clam dip.

Appetizer Cheese Spread
Makes 3½ cups

1 package (8 ounces) cream cheese
1 container (1 pound) cream-style cottage cheese
1 package (4 ounces) Camembert cheese
¼ cup grated Parmesan cheese
½ teaspoon seasoned salt
¼ teaspoon soy sauce
3 tablespoons light cream or table cream

1 Beat cream cheese until smooth in a large bowl; beat in all remaining ingredients. Chill.
2 When ready to serve, spoon into a small serving bowl; garnish with sprigs of parsley or strips of pimiento, if you wish. Place bowl in center of a large serving tray; surround with crisp crackers, party-size breads, and carrot and celery sticks.

Twin Cheese Molds
Makes 12 servings

2 cups grated sharp Cheddar cheese (½ pound)
4 tablespoons (½ stick) butter or margarine
1 teaspoon Worcestershire sauce
1 package (8 ounces) cream cheese, softened
1 can (2¼ or 3 ounces) deviled ham

1 Combine Cheddar cheese, butter or margarine and Worcestershire sauce in a medium-size bowl; beat until fluffy. Blend cream cheese and deviled ham until smooth in a second bowl.
2 Pack each mixture into an about 2-cup size paper cup, smoothing top even. Chill both several hours or overnight.
3 When ready to serve, snip rim of each cup and gently peel off paper; invert cheese molds onto a serving plate. Frame with assorted crisp crackers.

Pecan-Cheese Log
Stripes of pecans add a pretty trim and pleasing crunch to this zippy starter.
Makes 12 servings

1 package (8 ounces) cream cheese, softened
1 cup grated Swiss cheese (4 ounces)
1 cup crumbled blue cheese
½ teaspoon liquid red pepper seasoning
¼ cup chopped pecans

1 Blend cream cheese, Swiss cheese, blue cheese, and liquid red pepper seasoning in a medium-size bowl. Chill until firm enough to handle.

TWIN CHEESE MOLDS

Turn them into conversation-piece "candles." For the trims, cut tiny stars from pimiento with a truffle cutter and wicks from thin slices of carrot. Paper-cup molds give them their tall chunky shape.

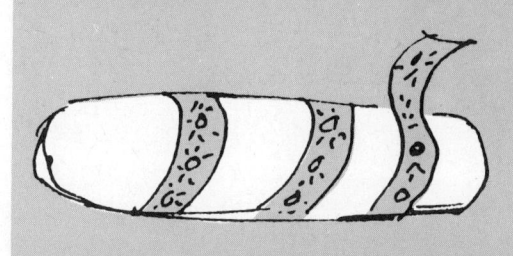

PECAN-CHEESE LOG

Give it a pretty striped dress this way: Press strips of foil diagonally around log after shaping, then roll in chopped nuts. Chill again; peel off foil. Another time, use sesame seeds in place of nuts.

2 Shape into an 8-inch-long log; wrap in waxed paper, foil, or transparent wrap and chill again until firm.
3 To make spiral trim, unwrap log; press ½-inch-wide strips of foil or wax paper diagonally, 1 inch apart, over top and side. Roll log in chopped pecans; chill again.
4 When ready to serve, carefully peel off paper; place log on a serving plate. Frame with assorted crisp crackers, if you wish.

87

Rosy Hungarian Spread
Makes about 1 cup

2 packages (3 ounces each) cream cheese, softened
2 tablespoons capers
1 tablespoon caraway seeds
1 tablespoon paprika

¼ cup dairy sour cream
½ clove garlic, crushed
1 teaspoon grated onion
¼ teaspoon liquid red pepper seasoning

Beat all ingredients with a fork or whirl in an electric blender until creamy-smooth. Use as a spread for rye rounds or crackers.

Pâté Continental

It's fussy to fix, but making ahead is a must to allow for baking loaf, chilling, and coating with sparkly gelatin.
Bake at 350° for 1½ hours. Makes 8 servings

1 pound beef liver
½ pound chicken livers
1 medium-size onion, chopped (½ cup)
2 tablespoons butter or margarine
¼ cup water
1 envelope instant chicken broth or 1 chicken-bouillon cube
2 eggs, beaten
¼ teaspoon ground allspice
¼ teaspoon leaf thyme, crumbled
5 slices bacon
    Beef Aspic (recipe follows)
1 hard-cooked egg, shelled

1 Snip out any large tubelike membranes from beef liver; cut into chunks. Halve chicken livers; snip out any veiny parts or skin.
2 Put both meats through a food chopper, using a fine blade; place in a medium-size bowl.
3 Sauté onion in butter or margarine until soft in a small frying pan; stir in water and chicken broth or bouillon cube; heat to boiling, crushing bouillon cube, if used, with a spoon; stir into liver mixture with eggs, allspice, and thyme.
4 Place 3 slices of the bacon in a loaf pan, 5x3x2; spoon in liver mixture; top with remaining bacon. Cover pan tightly with foil.
5 Set in a baking pan on oven shelf; pour boiling water into pan to depth of about an inch.
6 Bake in moderate oven (350°) 1½ hours, or until loaf starts to pull away from sides of pan; remove from pan of water; take off foil. Cool loaf, then chill overnight.
7 Make Beef Aspic.
8 Peel bacon from top of loaf; loosen loaf around edges with a knife; invert onto a plate; peel off remaining bacon. Wash pan and dry well.
9 Pour ¼ cup of the aspic into loaf pan; place

in a pan of ice and water to speed setting; chill just until sticky-firm.
10 While layer chills, halve hard-cooked egg lengthwise, cutting just through white. Slice yolk carefully; cut white into 8 or 10 tiny flower shapes with a truffle cutter. Arrange two of the egg-yolk slices and egg-white cutouts in a pretty pattern on sticky-firm aspic in pan; carefully pour in another ½ cup aspic; let set until sticky-firm.
11 Place pâté loaf over aspic layer in pan; pour in enough of the remaining aspic to fill pan to rim. Remove from ice and water; chill in refrigerator at least 4 hours, or until aspic is firm. Pour remaining aspic into a pan, 8x8x2; chill.
12 Just before serving, run a sharp-tip thin-blade knife around top of load, then dip pan very quickly in and out of hot water. Cover pan with a chilled serving plate; turn upside down; gently lift off pan.
13 Cut remaining aspic layer into tiny cubes; spoon around pâté loaf. Garnish with radish flowers and snips of radish leaves, if you wish, and serve with melba rounds or crackers. To make radish flowers, trim large radishes. Holding each, tip end up, cut lengthwise into 10 or 12 sections, cutting not quite to stem. Place in a bowl of ice and water until "petals" open.

BEEF ASPIC—Soften 1 envelope unflavored gelatin in ¾ cup cold water in a small saucepan; heat, stirring constantly, just until gelatin dissolves; remove from heat. Stir in 1 can condensed beef consommé and 2 tablespoons lemon juice. Cool.

Pâté Madrilène
Makes about 3 cups

1 envelope unflavored gelatin
1 can (about 13 ounces) consommé madrilène
2 hard-cooked eggs, shelled
2 cans (about 4 ounces each) liver spread
½ cup chopped toasted walnuts
1 tablespoon sweet pickle relish, drained
½ teaspoon salt
¼ teaspoon pepper

1 Soften gelatin in madrilène in a small saucepan. Heat, stirring constantly, until gelatin dissolves; remove from heat. Pour a half-inch-thick layer into a 3-cup bowl; chill just until sticky-firm. Cool remaining gelatin mixture in saucepan at room temperature.
2 Cut up eggs, then press through a sieve into

cooled gelatin mixture in saucepan; beat in liver spread, walnuts, relish, salt, and pepper until well-blended.

3 Pour over sticky-firm gelatin layer in bowl; chill several hours, or overnight, until firm.

4 When ready to serve, loosen pâté around edge with a knife; turn out onto a serving plate. Garnish top with sliced pimiento-stuffed olives, if you wish. Surround mold with crisp crackers.

NOTE: To toast walnuts, simmer in boiling water to cover in a small saucepan 3 minutes; drain. Spread in a single layer in a shallow baking pan. Heat in moderate oven (350°) 15 minutes.

NIBBLES

Popcorn Nibbles

Pop corn the skillet way. Heap a big bowl with snowy kernels, toss in one of these seasoners—and munch away!
Makes 8 generous cupfuls.

1 Measure 2 to 3 tablespoons vegetable oil and ½ cup popping corn into a large heavy skillet with tight-fitting cover.

2 Cover; heat slowly. When you hear the first pop, start shaking skillet gently and continue until popping stops.

Salt Dress-Ups

Popcorn worth its salt takes to all of the flavored varieties as well as regular table salt. Another twist: Twirl table salt in an electric blender until it's powdery fine, then sprinkle over corn. It sticks to the corn better, coats it more evenly.

Buttery Boosters

Treat freshly popped corn the same as salad greens and coat—not drown—in butter. Each of these seasoners makes enough for 8 cups popped corn.

1 Lemon Butter—Stir 1 tablespoon lemon juice into ¼ cup melted butter or margarine, pour over corn, and toss.

2 Dill Butter—Drizzle ¼ cup melted butter or margarine over corn, sprinkle with 2 teaspoons dill weed, and toss.

3 Sesame Brown Butter—Melt ¼ cup butter or margarine with 1 tablespoon sesame seeds over medium heat in a small frying pan. Continue heating, shaking pan often, just until butter foams up and turns golden. Pour over corn and toss.

4 Parmesan Butter—Stir 1 tablespoon grated Parmesan cheese into ¼ cup melted butter or margarine, pour over corn, and toss.

5 Curry Butter—Stir 1 teaspoon curry powder into ¼ cup melted butter or margarine, pour over corn, and toss.

6 Cinnamon Butter—Stir 1 tablespoon cinnamon-sugar into ¼ cup melted butter or margarine, pour over corn, and toss.

7 Barbecue Butter—Stir 1 teaspoon bottled barbecue sauce into ¼ cup melted butter or margarine, pour over corn and toss.

8 Paprika Butter—Stir ¼ teaspoon seasoned salt and ¼ teaspoon paprika into ¼ cup melted butter or margarine, then pour over corn and toss.

9 Garlic Butter—Stir ½ teaspoon garlic salt into ¼ cup melted butter or margarine, pour over corn and toss.

10 Onion Butter—Stir ½ teaspoon onion salt into ¼ cup melted butter or margarine, pour over corn and toss.

11 Chili Butter—Stir 1 teaspoon chili powder and ⅛ teaspoon garlic salt into ¼ cup melted butter or margarine, add a few drops liquid red pepper seasoning, if you wish, pour over corn and toss.

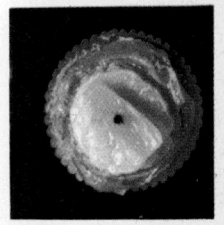

CANAPÉS AND HORS D´OEUVRES

Scandinavian Canapés

Virtually everything Scandinavians put their hands to is artistic, so it's not surprising that their canapés are mini masterpieces. To make those pictured here, butter slices of day-old bread and then cut them into rounds with a small cooky cutter or shot glass. Assemble the canapés using the ingredients listed in the photograph or create your own works of art, drawing upon your supermarket's vast array of cold cuts, savory spreads, mixes and deli-type salads. It's *that* easy.

Party Canapés

Fix these fancies ahead and freeze, ready for a party or drop-in guests.
Makes 2 dozen

4 tablespoons soft margarine
1 package (3 or 4 ounces) cream cheese

89

parsley
Swedish caviar
anchovy
hardboiled egg
salted butter

parsley
sweet onions
Swedish salami
salted butter

dill
capers
cream cheese
Nova Scotia salmon
salted butter

dill
mayonnaise
tiny shrimp
salted butter

mayonnaise
chopped parsley
sweet relish
smoked ham
salted butter

chopped parsley
tomato
pickled cucumber
Danish liver pâté
salted butter
decorative
toothpick

½ teaspoon Worcestershire sauce
2 hard-cooked eggs, shelled
3 slices white bread
3 slices whole wheat bread

1 Blend margarine, cream cheese, and Worcestershire sauce until smooth in a medium-size bowl; spoon half into a second bowl.
2 Halve eggs; remove yolks; press through a sieve and blend into mixture in one bowl. Cover bowl and set aside with whites for decorating canapés.
3 Trim crusts from bread; cut out 12 rounds with a 1½-inch cutter from 3 slices; cut 12 diamond shapes from remaining slices. Spread each with plain cheese mixture. Decorate and freeze.

How To Decorate and Freeze:
1 To decorate: Fill a cake-decorating set with cream-cheese-egg mixture; fit with star tip; pipe an edging around each canapé.
2 Garnish each with small whole shrimps, slivers of smoked salmon rolled up, bits of king crab meat or lobster, sliced stuffed green or ripe olives, capers, cut-up gherkins, diced pimiento, small pickled onions or diced hard-cooked egg white.
3 To freeze: Place canapés in a single layer in a large shallow pan; cover tightly with transparent wrap; freeze. When frozen, pack no more than two layers deep with transparent wrap between in boxes until ready to use. Plan to use frozen canapés within two weeks.
4 To thaw: Remove canapés from freezer 1 hour before serving;place in a single layer; let stand at room temperature.

Radish Crisps
Pungent parsley and nippy-crisp radish slices top circles of buttered bread.
Makes 4 dozen

24 thin slices white bread (about 1½ loaves)
 8 tablespoons (1 stick) butter or margarine, softened
 1 bunch radishes (about 12), trimmed and sliced thin
　Parsley

1 Cut 2 rounds from each slice of bread with a 2-inch cutter; spread rounds with butter or margarine, using about a half teaspoonful for each.
2 Arrange in a single layer on a cooky sheet or large tray lined with a damp towel. Place 2 radish slices, overlapping, on top of each round; trim with a sprig of parsley. Cover with waxed paper, foil, or transparent wrap; chill.

Tips for the hostess: Radish and parsley topping will stay fresh and crisp tor about 2 hours. For serving 100, make 3 times the recipe.

Artichoke-Egg Boats
Egg salad fills tiny "shells" of marinated artichokes for these different nibbles.
Makes about 2½ dozen

1 jar (6 ounces) marinated artichoke hearts
2 hard-cooked eggs, shelled and sieved
2 tablespoons bottled tartare sauce
　Pitted ripe olives, cut lengthwise into slivers

1 Drain artichoke hearts; split any large ones to make boat-shape shells.
2 Blend sieved eggs and tartare sauce in a small bowl; spoon into artichoke shells; garnish each with a sliver of olive.
Hostess tip: Put these morsels together about an hour ahead. Arrange in a single layer on a tray, cover, and chill.

WHEN YOU DECORATE AND FREEZE PARTY CANAPES

Pipe on a ruftly edging or rosettes with a cake-decorating set and add the toppers of your choice. Place canapés in a single layer in a pan, cover, and freeze. Then, to save freezer space, stack them—only two layers deep—with transparent wrap between and return to freezer until ready to use.

Stuffed Celery

Zippy cheese spread fills bite-size pieces of celery for this crunchy appetizer.
Makes 2 dozen

 1 package (3 or 4 ounces) cream cheese, softened
 ½ teaspoon Worcestershire sauce
 ½ teaspoon lemon juice
 1 tablespoon finely chopped pistachio nuts
24 one-inch-long pieces of celery

1 Blend cream cheese. Worcestershire sauce, and lemon juice until smooth in a small bowl; stir in pistachio nuts.
2 Fill hollows of each piece of celery; garnish with pistachio nuts, if you wish.

Button Mushroom Cups

A real delicacy! Mushroom caps are sautéed first, then heaped with pâté filling.
Makes 1 dozen

12 medium-size fresh mushrooms (about ½ pound)
 1 tablespoon vegetable oil
 2 teaspoons grated onion
 ¼ cup liver pâté (from a 4½-ounce can)
 2 tablespoons chopped parsley
 3 cherry tomatoes, quartered lengthwise

1 Wipe mushrooms well with a damp cloth. Remove stems and chop. Set aside for making filling in Step 3.
2 Sauté mushroom caps in vegetable oil in a medium-size frying pan 2 minutes, or just until heated through; place on a plate.
3 Sauté chopped stems with grated onion just until soft in same pan; place in a small bowl; stir in liver pâté and parsley.
4 Pile into mushroom caps. Garnish each with a quartered cherry tomato. Chill until serving time.

Deviled Egg Rounds

Popular deviled eggs go appetizer fancy! Toast base is the packaged kind.
Makes 16 rounds

 4 eggs, hard-cooked and shelled
 6 tablespoons mayonnaise or salad dressing
 2 tablespoons sweet-pickle relish
 ¼ teaspoon salt

 ¼ teaspoon dry mustard
   Few drops liquid red pepper seasoning
16 melba toast rounds
   Parsley

1 Cut eggs crosswise into thin slices; remove yolks and press through a sieve into a small bowl.
2 Set aside 16 of the prettiest white "rings" for Step 3, then chop remaining and add to sieved egg yolk. Stir in 4 tablespoons of the mayonnaise or salad dressing, relish, salt, mustard, and liquid red pepper seasoning.
3 Spread remaining 2 tablespoons mayonnaise or salad dressing on toast rounds; place an egg-white ring on each; spoon yolk mixture on top. Garnish with parsley. Chill until serving time.

Spicy Stuffed Eggs

No one seems to tire of these favorites—and they always add such a pretty touch.
Makes 6 servings

 7 hard-cooked eggs, shelled
 2 tablespoons mayonnaise or salad dressing
 1 teaspoon prepared mustard
   Salt and pepper
12 capers

1 Halve 6 of the eggs lengthwise; scoop out yolks. Press yolks and remaining whole egg through a sieve into a small bowl.
2 Stir in mayonnaise or salad dressing and mustard; season with salt and pepper.
3 Pile back into whites; garnish each with a caper. Chill.

Cheese Twists

Sharp Cheddar gives these golden pastrylike sticks a mellow tang.
Bake at 425° for 10 minutes. Makes 4 dozen

 1 cup sifted all-purpose flour
1½ teaspoons baking powder
 ½ teaspoon salt
 2 tablespoons butter or margarine
 ½ cup grated sharp Cheddar cheese
 ⅓ cup cold water

1 Sift flour, baking powder, and salt into a medium-size bowl; cut in butter or margarine and cheese with a pastry blender until mixture is crumbly. Sprinkle water over; mix lightly with a fork just until mixture holds together and leaves side of bowl clean.
2 Roll out to a rectangle, 12x10, on a lightly floured pastry cloth or board. Divide in half lengthwise, then cut each half crosswise into

½-inch-wide strips. Lift strips, one at a time, and carefully twist. Place, 1 inch apart, on ungreased cooky sheets.

3 Bake in hot oven (425°) 10 minutes, or until lightly golden. Remove carefully and cool on wire racks.

●

Swiss Crisps

One bite of these hot crusty little cheese cubes just coaxes you into having another.
Makes about 1 dozen

    1 egg
    ¾ cup fine dry bread crumbs
    ½ pound Swiss cheese, cut into 1-inch cubes
        Shortening or vegetable oil for frying

1 Beat egg with 1 tablespoon of the bread crumbs in a small bowl. Place remaining bread crumbs in a pie plate.

2 Dip cheese cubes into egg mixture, then into bread crumbs to coat well.

3 Melt enough shortening or pour in vegetable oil to make a 3-inch depth in an electric deep-fat fryer or large saucepan; heat to 380°.

4 Fry cheese cubes, a few at a time, 1 minute, or until crisp and golden. Lift out with a slotted spoon; drain well on paper toweling. Keep warm until all are cooked.

●

Sesame Puffs

Crisp nibbles bake in flaky layers much like puff pastry.
Bake at 400° for 15 minutes. Makes 4 dozen

    1½ cups sifted all-purpose flour
    1 teaspoon garlic salt
    ½ cup (1 stick) butter or margarine
    ½ cup dairy sour cream
        Sesame seeds

1 Sift flour and garlic salt into a medium-size bowl; cut in butter or margarine with a pastry blender until mixture is crumbly.

2 Stir in sour cream lightly with a fork just until pastry holds together and leaves side of bowl clean; wrap in wax paper or transparent wrap. Chill at least 4 hours or overnight.

3 Roll out pastry, ¼ inch thick, on a lightly floured pastry cloth or board; cut into rounds or fancy shapes with a floured 1½-inch cutter. Place on ungreased cooky sheets. Brush cutouts with water; sprinkle with sesame seeds.

4 Bake in hot oven (400°) 15 minutes, or until puffed and golden. Remove from cooky sheets to wire racks; cool.

NOTE: Puffs may be made a day or two ahead and stored in a tightly covered container so they'll stay crisp. Serve cold, or reheat just before serving time.

●

Midget Tacos

Makes 18 servings

    1 small firm ripe avocado
    1 small tomato
    1 small onion, chopped (¼ cup)
    1 small clove of garlic, minced
    2 teaspoons lemon juice
    ¼ teaspoon liquid red pepper seasoning

Celery chunks, cherry tomatoes, carrot curls all make handy containers for cocktail dips.

93

1 teaspoon salt
¼ teaspoon chili powdor
9 tortillas (from an 11-ounce can)
Vegetable oil or shortening for frying
1½ cups shredded iceberg lettuce
1 hard-cooked egg yolk, sieved

1 Halve avocado; peel and pit. Mash with a fork in a medium-size bowl. Peel tomato and halve; seed half, then chop fine; stir into avocado with onion, garlic, lemon juice, liquid red pepper seasoning, salt, and chili powder. Chill a half hour to season. Cut remaining half tomato into tiny triangles for garnish.

2 Quarter each tortilla. Pour vegetable oil or melt enough shortening in a small saucepan to make a 1-inch depth; heat. Holding tortilla quarters, one at a time, with tongs to form U shapes, fry in hot oil several seconds; lift out and drain on paper toweling.

3 Place a thin layer of shredded lettuce in each tortilla; top with a rounded teaspoonful avocado mixture; sprinkle with sieved egg yolk. Tuck a tiny tomato triangle into each end.

●

Pizza Pickups
Bake at 400° for 5 minutes. Makes 24 appetizers

24 sesame wafers
 1 package (4 ounces) sliced prosciutto, cut in 24 pieces
 4 small tomatoes, each cut in 6 thin slices
½ teaspoon garlic salt
 Grated Parmesan cheese
 4 slices provolone cheese
12 pimiento-stuffed olives, halved

1 Place sesame wafers in a single layer in a jelly-roll pan. Top each with prosciutto, folding slices, if needed, to fit. Place tomato slices over prosciutto. Sprinkle garlic salt, then Parmesan cheese over tomatoes.

2 Cut each slice of provolone cheese in 6 wedges; place over tomatoes; top with olive halves.

3 Bake in hot oven (400°) 5 minutes, or until cheese melts. Serve hot.

●

Rumaki
Makes two dozen

12 chicken livers, halved at the natural separation
24 thin slivers water chestnut
12 slices bacon, cut in half

Midget Tacos and Guacamole are a tasty party twosome.

1½ cups Japanese soy sauce
1 clove garlic, minced
1 cup light brown sugar

1 Make a small incision in center of each piece of chicken liver and insert a sliver of water chestnut. Wrap each with a half strip of bacon and secure with a toothpick.
2 Mix soy sauce and garlic, add livers, cover and marinate in the refrigerator several hours.
3 Remove livers from marinade, roll lightly in brown sugar and broil until bacon is crisp. Serve hot.

Finger Drumsticks
Bake at 400° for 1 hour and 10 minutes. Makes 12 servings

3 pounds small chicken wings (about 15)
½ cup sugar
3 tablespoons cornstarch
1 teaspoon salt

½ teaspoon ground ginger
¼ teaspoon pepper
¾ cup water
⅓ cup lemon juice
¼ cup soy sauce

1 Singe chicken wings, if needed. Cut off tips and discard. Divide each wing in half by cutting through joint with a sharp knife. Place in a single layer on rack in broiler pan.
2 Bake in hot oven (400°), turning once, 30 minutes.
3 Mix sugar, cornstarch, salt, ginger, and pepper in a small saucepan; stir in water, lemon juice, and soy sauce. Cook, stirring constantly, until mixture thickens and boils 3 minutes. Brush part over chicken wings.
4 Continue baking, turning and brushing several times with remaining lemon mixture, 40 minutes, or until richly glazed.
5 When ready to serve, place in a chafing dish or keep-hot server. Frame with a ring of thin lemon slices, if you wish. Serve hot.

As welcome at a cocktail party as at a picnic—Finger Drumsticks, these fried simply without a soy glaze.

Chicken Canapés
Makes 12 servings

1 can (5 ounces) chicken spread
2 packages (3 ounces each) cream cheese with chives
½ teaspoon salt
¼ teaspoon pepper
24 slices party-size rye bread
4 tablespoons (½ stick) butter or margarine
1 medium-size cucumber

1 Blend chicken spread with cheese, salt, and pepper in a small bowl.
2 Spread each slice of bread with ½ teaspoon butter or margarine.
3 Cut 24 thin even slices from cucumber; cut remaining cucumber into tiny wedges for garnish. Spoon 1 teaspoonful chicken mixture on each cucumber slice; place on bread. Garnish each with two wedges of cucumber, butterfly style.

Bacon Wands
Bake at 400° for 10 minutes. Makes 12 sticks

12 slices bacon
12 very thin bread sticks

1 Preheat oven.
2 Wrap bacon, spiral fashion, around the bread sticks; place, ends of bacon down, on rack on broiler pan.
3 Place broiler pan in oven; bake in hot oven (400°) for 10 minutes, or until bacon is crisply cooked. Serve warm.

Fancy Franks
Bake at 400° for 15 minutes. Makes 32 appetizers

1 package piecrust mix
1 can (8 ounces) sauerkraut
¼ cup shredded sharp Cheddar cheese
¼ teaspoon liquid red pepper seasoning
2 teaspoons prepared mustard
1 package (about 5 ounces) tiny frankfurters, cut crosswise into halves
Milk

1 Prepare piecrust mix, following label directions, or make pastry from your favorite two-crust recipe.
2 Drain sauerkraut very well, then pat between paper toweling to remove excess moisture; chop fine. Combine with cheese and red pepper seasoning in a small bowl.
3 Roll out half the pastry to an about-12-inch square on a lightly floured pastry cloth or board. Cut out 2½-inch rounds with a biscuit cutter; remove extra pastry. Spread rounds *lightly* with prepared mustard and place a frankfurter half in center of each round; add 1 teaspoon sauerkraut mixture on end of each frankfurter. Lift sides of each pastry round and pinch together across top to enclose franks and kraut completely. Place on ungreased cooky sheet. Repeat with second half of pastry and reroll any trimming, if necessary, to make 32 rounds in all. Brush lightly with milk.
4 Bake in hot oven (400°) 15 minutes, or until pastry is very lightly browned. Serve warm.

Miniature Wiener Wellingtons
Bake at 375° for 10 minutes. Makes 16 servings

¼ pound piece liverwurst or Braunschweiger
2 tablespoons grated Parmesan cheese
½ teaspoon onion salt
2 packages (8 ounces each) cocktail frankfurters
2 packages (8 to a package) refrigerated crescent dinner rolls

1 Peel casing from liverwurst; slice meat into 8 rounds. Cut each round into 4 strips; trim strips, if needed, to fit into cocktail frankfurters.
2 Mix cheese and onion salt on waxed paper; roll each strip of liverwurst in cheese mixture.
3 Split each frankfurter almost to bottom; stuff with a strip of seasoned liverwurst; cut each in half.
4 Unroll crescent dough, one package at a time, into 2 rectangles; pinch together at perforations. Cut each rectangle crosswise into 16 one-inch-wide strips; wrap each around a half frankfurter. Repeat with remaining package of rolls. Place rolls, seam side down, on a cooky sheet.
5 Bake in moderate oven (375°) 10 minutes, or until golden. Serve hot.

Little Ham Kebabs
Bake loaf at 350° for 1 hour. Makes 30 servings

½ pound ham, ground
2 eggs
½ cup fine soda cracker crumbs
¼ cup milk

A skillful mix of colors, shapes, textures, flavors can make an hors d'oeuvre tray properly festive, party perfect.

2 tablespoons prepared horseradish-mustard
2 teaspoons grated onion
½ teaspoon salt
16 medium-size radishes
8 medium-size sweet pickles

1 Line a small loaf pan, 7x4x2, with foil, leaving a 1-inch overhang all around.
2 Combine ham, eggs, cracker crumbs, milk, horseradish-mustard, onion, and salt in a medium-size bowl; mix lightly until well-blended. Spoon into prepared pan; spread top even.
3 Bake in moderate oven (350°) 1 hour, or until firm and lightly browned on top. Loosen loaf around sides with a knife, then pull up on foil and lift from pan; place on a plate. Chill several hours, or until completely cold.
4 Trim radishes; slice each into 8 thin slices. Slice each pickle into 16 thin slices.
5 When ready to finish kebabs, peel foil from ham loaf; cut loaf into 8 slices, then each slice into 8 cubes. For each kebab, stack a radish and pickle slice, ham cube, pickle and radish slice; hold in place with a wooden pick. (Tip: For showy serving, halve a large grapefruit. Place halves on a parsley-lined plate; stick kebabs into grapefruit.)

Bitsy Burgers
Bake at 375° for 14 minutes. Makes 20 servings

1 pound ground beef
1 teaspoon seasoned salt
5 slices process American cheese
4 tablespoons (½ stick) butter or margarine
2 tablespoons prepared mustard
5 split hamburger buns
10 cherry tomatoes, sliced thin
8 small white onions, peeled and sliced thin

1 Mix ground beef and seasoned salt lightly in a small bowl; shape into 40 one-inch patties. Place in a single layer in a shallow baking pan.
2 Bake in moderate oven (375°) for 10 minutes.
3 Cut each cheese slice into 9 squares; place one over each meat patty. Bake 4 minutes longer, or until cheese melts slightly.
4 While meat cooks, blend butter or margarine and mustard in a cup. Toast hamburger buns in oven; spread with butter mixture; cut each half in 4 triangles.
5 When ready to serve, place each meat patty on a bun triangle; top with a slice each of tomato and onion; hold in place with a wooden pick. Serve hot.

97

APPETIZERS AND HORS D'OEUVRES

Deviled Riblets
Bake at 350° for 2 hours. Makes 12 servings

2 ½ pounds fresh spareribs
2 tablespoons lemon juice
2 tablespoons prepared mustard
1 package seasoned coating mix for pork
2 tablespoons chopped parsley

1 Have your meatman crack ribs into 1½-inch-long pieces. When ready to cook, cut apart and separate into ribs. Place in a single layer on rack in broiler pan.
2 Bake in moderate oven (350°), turning several times, 1½ hours; pour drippings from pan.
3 While ribs cook, mix lemon juice and mustard in a cup; brush half over ribs. Sprinkle with half of the coating mix.
4 Bake 15 minutes; turn ribs. Brush with remaining mustard mixture; sprinkle with remaining coating mix. Bake 15 minutes longer, or until crisp.
5 When ready to serve, arrange ribs in a chafing dish or keep-hot server; sprinkle with chopped parsley. Serve hot.

Little Clambakes
Bake at 400° for 5 minutes. Makes 4 dozen

1 package (8 ounces) cream cheese
1 can (8 ounces) minced clams
1 tablespoon bottled onion juice
½ teaspoon liquid red pepper seasoning
4 dozen buttery crackers
Paprika

1 Soften cheese in a medium-size bowl. Drain clams very well; add to cheese with onion juice and red pepper seasoning. Mix well to blend. (If making ahead, store, covered, in refrigerator.)
2 Just before serving, spread clam mixture on crackers, about 1 teaspoonful on each. Sprinkle lightly with paprika; place on large cooky sheets.
3 Bake in hot oven (400°) for 5 minutes, or just until heated through but not browned. Garnish with sliced black olives and watercress leaves, if you wish.

Petites Coquilles St.-Jacques
Makes 18 servings

½ pound fresh sea scallops
OR: ½ pound frozen sea scallops, thawed
2 tablespoons milk
3 tablespoons flour
4 tablespoons (½ stick) butter or margarine
2 teaspoons lemon juice
1 tablespoon minced parsley
1 tablespoon chopped pimiento

1 Cut scallops into tiny cubes; place in a medium-size bowl. Sprinkle milk over top, then flour; toss to coat well.
2 Heat 2 tablespoons of the butter or margarine in a medium-size frying pan; add scallops, tossing to coat well with butter. Cook just 3 minutes, or until lightly browned; remove from heat. Stir in lemon juice, parsley, and pimiento.
3 Heat remaining 2 tablespoons butter or margarine slowly until golden brown in a small frying pan; pour over scallops.
4 When ready to serve, spoon scallop mixture into heated tiny scallop shells. Serve hot.

Copenhagens
Tiny shrimps with a tart sauce perch atop slices of crisp water chestnuts.
Makes 4 dozen

1 can (5 ounces) water chestnuts
48 tiny cocktail shrimps (from a 3-ounce jar)
¼ cup mayonnaise or salad dressing
1 tablespoon chopped parsley
½ teaspoon lemon juice

1 Drain water chestnuts; cut each into about-⅛-inch-thick rounds with a sharp knife. Drain shrimps; place in a small bowl.
2 Blend mayonnaise or salad dressing, parsley, and lemon juice in a 1-cup measure. Place a dab on each water-chestnut slice; stand a shrimp on top.
Hostess tip: Have plenty of these nibbles ready in the refrigerator, for one just coaxes you into having another. If making more than one recipe, count on about 90 perfect shrimps from a 3-ounce jar.

Butterfly Shrimps
A special favorite with men, especially when served with a spicy dip.
Makes about 2 dozen

1 pound fresh or frozen large raw shrimps
Water
1 slice of lemon
1 tablespoon packaged shrimp spice
Bottled cocktail sauce or tartare sauce

1 Wash shrimps in colander under running cold water. (If frozen, they will separate easily and start to thaw.)
2 Holding each shrimp rounded-shell-side-down, break off feelers, then run your thumb

Marinated Shrimp, Tomato-Salmon Thimbles and Parsley Scallops pyramided on crushed ice.

under shell, bending shell back along side and easing shrimp out.

3 Make a shallow cut down curve of back with a sharp-point knife; lift out black line, or sand vein, with knife tip.

4 Drop shrimps into an about-1-inch depth of simmering water seasoned with lemon and shrimp spice in a large frying pan; cook about 5 minutes for fresh shrimps, 10 minutes for frozen, or just until tender.

5 Remove from water with a slotted spoon; place in a single layer in a shallow dish; cover and chill.

6 Serve with a dip of bottled cocktail sauce or tartare sauce.

Shrimp Newburg Tartlets

Bake shells at 400° for 15 minutes, then at 300° for 15 minutes. Makes 18 servings

1 package piecrust mix
4 jars (about 3 ounces each) cocktail shrimps, drained
4 tablespoons (½ stick) butter or margarine
1 tablespoon flour
½ teaspoon salt
¼ teaspoon pepper
Dash of ground nutmeg
1 cup light cream or table cream
1 egg yolk
2 tablespoons dry sherry

1 Prepare piecrust mix, following label directions, or make pastry from your favorite double-crust recipe.

2 Roll out, half at a time, ⅛ inch thick, on a lightly floured pastry cloth or board. Cut into rounds with a 2½-inch cutter; fit each into a tiny muffin-pan cup, pressing firmly against bottom and side. Reroll trimmings to make 36 shells in all. Prick shells well with a fork.

3 Bake in hot oven (400°) 15 minutes, or until golden. Remove carefully from pans; cool completely on wire racks.

4 Set aside 36 shrimps for garnish; place remainder in pastry shells. Set shells in a large shallow pan.

5 Melt butter or margarine in a small saucepan; stir in flour, salt, pepper, and nutmeg. Cook, stirring constantly, until bubbly. Stir in cream; continue cooking and stirring until sauce thickens and boils 1 minute.

6 Beat egg yolk in a small bowl; beat in about half of the hot sauce, then stir back into remaining sauce in pan. Cook, stirring constantly, 1 minute; stir in sherry. Spoon over shrimps in shells.

7 Bake in slow oven (300°) 15 minutes, or until hot. Garnish with saved shrimps. Serve hot.

Marinated Shrimp

Makes 8 to 10 servings

2 pounds shrimp, cooked, shelled and deveined
1 cup mayonnaise or salad dressing
¼ cup olive oil or vegetable oil
¼ cup chili sauce or catsup
1 clove garlic, crushed
1 small onion, grated

99

1 teaspoon celery seed
1 tablespoon minced fresh dill
OR: 1 teaspoon dillweed

Combine all ingredients, cover and chill several hours or overnight. To serve: mound in a large bowl and put out a small container of tooth-picks.

Mandarin Shrimp Sticks

If you make the curry dip ahead, reheat it slightly just before serving.
Makes 10 to 12 servings

2 teaspoons curry powder
2 tablespoons butter or margarine
1 tablespoon flour
2 teaspoons instant minced onion
½ teaspoon garlic salt
½ teaspoon sugar
1 envelope instant chicken broth
1 cup water
1 teaspoon lemon juice
1 pound shrimps, cooked and deveined
1 can (11 ounces) mandarin-orange segments, drained

1 Heat curry powder in butter or margarine in a small saucepan 1 minute. Stir in flour, onion, garlic salt, sugar, and chicken broth; cook, stirring constantly, until bubbly. Stir in water; continue cooking and stirring until sauce thickens and boils 1 minute; remove from heat. Stir in lemon juice; spoon into a small bowl.
2 Thread each shrimp and a mandarin-orange segment onto a wooden pick; serve with warm curry sauce.

Lobster Bites

They're easy as can be to get ready. Serve with a sauce or dip—or even plain.
Makes about 2 dozen

100

1 package (10 ounces) frozen South African lobster tails
1 tablespoon mixed pickling spices
1 slice of onion
½ teaspoon salt
Lemon juice
Bottled cocktail sauce or tartare sauce

1 Cook lobster tails with pickling spices, onion, and salt, following label directions. Drain and cool completely.
2 With scissors, cut through and remove the thick membrane on underside of shell. Take out lobster meat by peeling hard shell back with

fingers of one hand and pulling meat toward you with the other.
3 Cut meat into ½-inch-thick slices; sprinkle with lemon juice. Cover; chill.
4 Serve with a dip of bottled cocktail sauce or tartare sauce.

Deviled Crab Croutons

Fix toast squares and crab salad ahead, ready to put together just before serving.
Makes 4 dozen

1 can (about 7 ounces) white crab meat
1 tablespoon lemon juice
2 drops liquid red pepper seasoning
¼ cup very finely diced celery
1 tablespoon chopped parsley
⅓ cup mayonnaise or salad dressing
¼ teaspoon soy sauce
48 one-inch-square croutons
Seedless green grapes, cut lengthwise into slivers

1 Drain crab meat well; toss with lemon juice and liquid red pepper seasoning in a small bowl. Chill about 15 minutes, then drain well again.
2 Stir in celery, parsley, mayonnaise or salad dressing, and soy sauce. Spoon onto croutons; garnish each with a sliver of grape.
Hostess tip: To make croutons, trim crusts from slices of white bread; cut each slice into about-1-inch squares. Place in a single layer on a cooky sheet. Toast in moderate oven (350°) 15 minutes, or until crisp. Cool, then store in a tightly covered container until ready to use. Crab salad recipe makes about 1 cup, so chill any left over for sandwich filling.

Hot Sea-Food Hors D'Oeuvre

Let everyone spear his own shrimp, scallop, or codfish ball, then dunk into sauce.
Makes 12 servings

4 tablespoons (½ stick) butter or margarine
1 pound frozen deveined shelled raw shrimps
1 clove of garlic, minced
1 pound fresh or frozen raw sea scallops
1 package (8 ounces) frozen cooked codfish balls
1 jar (about 6 ounces) hollandaise sauce
1 jar (about 12 ounces) cocktail sauce
2 tablespoons chopped parsley
Paprika

1 Melt 2 tablespoons butter or margarine in medium-size frying pan. (Save remaining 2 tablespoons for Step 3.) Add frozen shrimps and garlic; simmer, stirring often, 20 to 25 minutes,

or just until shrimps are tender; remove from heat but keep hot.

2 While shrimps cook, wash fresh scallops under running cold water; drain. (Or partly thaw frozen scallops, following label directions.) Cut any large scallops in bite-size pieces.

3 Melt saved 2 tablespoons butter or margarine in second medium-size frying pan; add scallops. Cook slowly, stirring often, 5 to 8 minutes, or until tender; keep hot.

4 Heat codfish balls, following label directions; keep hot.

5 Heat hollandaise sauce just until piping-hot in top of double boiler over simmering water. (Don't let water boil.) Heat cocktail sauce to boiling in small saucepan.

6 When ready to serve, pile shrimps, scallops, and codfish balls in separate mounds in chafing dish; sprinkle parsley over shrimps and paprika over scallops. Spoon hollandaise and cocktail sauces into separate small bowls. Remember to set out cocktail picks for spearing and dunking.

Lobster Baskets

Hollowed-out bread cubes hold mellow seafood salad.

Bake baskets at 350° for 12 minutes. Makes 24 servings of 2 each

1 loaf (1 pound) unsliced firm white bread
4 tablespoons (½ stick) butter or margarine, melted
1 can (5 ounces) lobster meat
1 pimiento
3 tablespoons mayonnaise or salad dressing
2 teaspoons lemon juice

1 Trim end crusts from bread; cut loaf crosswise into 6 one-inch-thick slices. Trim slices to 3-inch squares, then cut each into 9 small squares. With a sharp-tip knife, hollow out squares to make tiny baskets. Brush with melted butter or margarine; place on a cooky sheet.

2 Bake in moderate oven (350°) 12 minutes, or until golden; cool.

3 Drain lobster and pimiento; chop both fine. Mix with mayonnaise or salad dressing and lemon juice in a small bowl.

4 About an hour before serving, spoon into breadbaskets, using about 1 teaspoonful for each. Garnish with cucumber wedges, if you wish.

Parsley Scallops

Bottled salad dressing is their peppy seasoner.
Makes about 2 dozen

½ pound fresh or frozen sea scallops
1 slice of onion
1 slice of lemon
½ teaspoon salt
2 cups water
1 tablespoon bottled Italian salad dressing
¼ cup chopped parsley
1 lime, halved and sliced thin

1 Wash fresh scallops under running cold water or partly thaw frozen ones; cut into quarters.

2 Combine onion and lemon slices, salt, and water in a medium-size saucepan; heat to boiling; add scallops; cover. Remove from heat; let stand 5 minutes, then drain.

3 Place scallops in a small bowl; drizzle Italian dressing over; toss to mix. Cover; chill.

4 When ready to serve, dip scallops into parsley to coat; place each on a wooden pick and stick into a half slice of lime.

Tomato-Salmon Thimbles

Makes 24 servings

1 can (8 ounces) salmon
¼ cup mayonnaise or salad dressing
1 tablespoon chili sauce
2 teaspoons grated onion
2 teaspoons lemon juice
½ teaspoon dillweed
½ teaspoon Worcestershire sauce
⅛ teaspoon salt
Few drops liquid red pepper seasoning
2 containers cherry tomatoes, stemmed

1 Drain liquid from salmon; remove bones and skin, then flake salmon into a medium-size bowl.

2 Blend mayonnaise or salad dressing, chili sauce, onion, lemon juice, dillweed, Worcestershire sauce, salt, and red pepper seasoning in a cup; fold into salmon.

3 Cut a thin slice from the blossom end of each tomato; hollow out insides slightly with the ¼ teaspoon of a measuring-spoon set. Stuff each with 1 teaspoonful of the salmon mixture. Stand on a serving plate; chill.

4 Before serving, garnish each with parsley.

101

BEVERAGES

BEVERAGES

BEVERAGES:
APPETIZER DRINKS,
COFFEE AND TEA, MILK
DRINKS, FRUIT DRINKS,
PARTY PUNCHES

Hot or cold, tart or sweet, thick or thin, bland or spiked—each has a place. What cools a sultry summer day faster than a frosty glass of lemonade, for example, or warms a blustery December afternoon quicker than a chocolatey cup of cocoa, or gets the party off to a livelier start than a well-laced punch, or says "Merry Christmas" more deliciously than a festive, foamy bowl of eggnog? You'll find all the recipes here. And many, many more as well as suggestions for giving drinks pretty party dress.

103

By way of introduction to the collection of beverage recipes that follows, a luscious line-up of milk and fruit based coolers wearing high-fashion garnishes.

Let the server double as a trim

Just plain, or simply decorated with a sprig of mint, a scooped-out orange is a party-dresser and makes a colorful cup. Save the fruit to dice and add to salad or dessert

Give grapes a sugary coat

Break off dainty bunches and dip into an egg white beaten slightly with about a half teaspoon of water, then into granulated sugar, turning to coat well. Set aside on paper toweling until dry. Drape over rim of glass

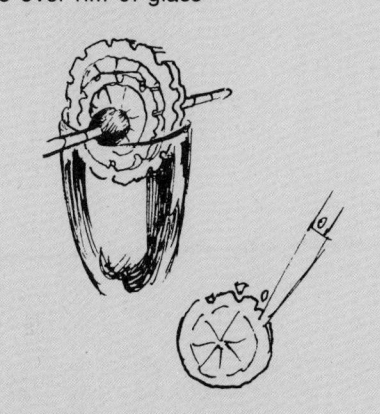

Freeze trims by the trayful

Here's how to make a variety of bright garnishes at one time: Place a berry; cherry; wedge of orange, lemon, or lime; or a thin strip of peel in each compartment of an ice-cube tray. Fill with water and freeze as usual

Make a catchy cartwheel

Spinning kebabs look summery-gay and are so easy to make: Just notch orange and lemon or lime slices around the edge, and thread with a maraschino cherry onto a sipper straw

104

Go gay with kebabs

Let your imagination be your guide, for all kinds, colors, sizes, and shapes of fruits—even candy for youngsters—inspire many good-to-eat dress-ups. Thread your choices on drinking straws or stirrer sticks, and make them long or short to fit into a pitcher or glass. Combinations shown here: Watermelon and honeydew balls; cut-up kumquats and chunks of banana rolled in lemon juice and coconut; marshmallows on a candy stick; orange slices and whole strawberries; and raspberries, pear rounds, and blueberries

APPETIZER DRINKS

Tomato Cocktail
Makes 6 servings

1 can (about 1 quart 14 ounces) tomato juice
  Juice of ½ lemon
1 teaspoon grated onion
1 teaspoon Worcestershire sauce
⅛ teaspoon liquid red pepper seasoning
  Salt to taste

Stir all ingredients to mix; chill and serve as an appetizer.

●

Tomato Bouillon
Makes 6 servings

1 can (about 1 pint 2 ounces) tomato juice
1 can (10¾ ounces) condensed beef bouillon
1 teaspoon lemon juice
¼ teaspoon garlic powder
⅛ teaspoon liquid red pepper seasoning

Stir all ingredients to mix; serve hot or cold as an appetizer.

●

Tomato-Clam Cocktail
Makes 6 servings

1 can (about 1 pint 2 ounces) tomato juice
2 bottles (8 ounces each) clam juice
2 teaspoons lemon juice or dill pickle juice
⅛ teaspoon liquid red pepper seasoning

Stir all ingredients well; chill and serve as an appetizer.

●

Curried Clam Cocktail
Curry and lemon give a fresh flavor lift to this jiffy-fix special.
Makes 4 servings

2 bottles (8 ounces each) clam juice
1 can (8 ounces) tomato sauce
1 tablespoon lemon juice
½ teaspoon curry powder
  Crushed ice

1 Combine clam juice, tomato sauce, lemon juice, and curry powder in a 4-cup shaker; shake to mix well.
2 Pour over crushed ice in glasses; serve plain or garnish with a slice of lemon, if you wish.

COFFEE AND TEA

COFFEE

Tips on Buying:
   No one variety of coffee bean has all of the characteristics for superb flavor, aroma and body. Packers carefully select and skillfully blend green coffees, often from several countries, into their own special recipe for a perfect brew. This is why no two brands ever taste the same.
   Many supermarkets carry as many as 90 different coffee items: whole-bean coffee, ground, instant, freeze-dried, decaffeinated, chicory-or-spice-flavored; coffee in vacuum cans, bags, glass jars or reusable containers with all kinds of easy-open conveniences. The best coffee for you is what tastes best to you. You'll be most satisfied if you experiment with several brands first, pick the one you prefer, and stick to it.

Tips on Storing:
   Buy often and only what you can use within a week after it's opened, for, like many foods, coffee deteriorates with age. Once opened, store coffee in a clean air-tight can or canister. Exposure to the air makes coffee lose much of its fresh flavor and after about 10 days, it will take on a disagreeable staleness. This doesn't mean you should bypass "specials" on vacuum-packed coffee, for as long as it's unopened, it will last almost indefinitely.

About Instant and Freeze-Dried Coffees:
   These convenience foods rate high on the hit parade of beverages, and a United States Department of Agriculture study shows that a cup of instant coffee costs about half as much as one made with the ground variety. Among the choices are regular instant and freeze-dried coffee, caffeine-free, espresso and other types of instant containing chicory, all packed in glass jars from two to 16 ounces. As a general rule, figure about 30 servings from a two-ounce jar, and do remember to use both instant and freeze-dried coffees as flavorings for all kinds of dishes. Be sure to recap the jar tightly after opening to keep out moisture and always use a dry spoon when measuring. The best ways to prepare these convenience coffees are as labels direct.

Answers to Questions Often Asked about Coffee:

Q. *What is chicory?*
A. Contrary to popular belief, it is not coffee but the roasted ground root of the chicory plant. It's sometimes used to flavor coffee

105

or as a coffee substitute. The label will tell you if chicory has been added.

Q. *Is there any way to stretch coffee?*
A. No, there isn't, and you'll only be disappointed if you try to be a miser. Using too little coffee only makes a watered-down brew.

Q. *What is green coffee?*
A. Surprisingly enough, "green" refers to unroasted coffee beans, not to their color. Green beans range from bluish gray to gray to yellow.

Q. *What is decaffeinated coffee?*
A. It is pure coffee from which nearly all of the caffein (a mild stimulant) has been removed before roasting. It comes in ground and instant forms.

Q. *Should soap be used on a coffeepot?*
A. Yes, indeed. As coffee brews, the oils coat the inside of the pot and turn rancid if not cleaned off completely. It's good practice to scrub, rinse, and dry the pot after each use.

Tips for Making Perfect Coffee:
The perfect cup of coffee is . . . sparklingly clear . . . amber to medium brown in color . . . of good bracing aroma . . . of fresh mellow flavor with no stale or bitter taste. To make:
• Keep coffeepot spotless; store unassembled so that air can circulate around component parts.
• Use fresh, good quality coffee, suiting the grind to your particular coffeemaker, and use freshly drawn, soft cold water.
• Measure grounds and water precisely, using the Coffee-Making Chart that follows as a guide.
• Brew coffee carefully, following directions provided by manufacturer of your coffeemaker.
• NEVER LET THE COFFEE BOIL.

The Different Grinds of Coffee:
Regular Grind (the coarsest)—for *percolators.*
Drip Grind (medium fine)—for *drip pots* and *vacuum coffeemakers.*
Fine Grind (the finest)—for *vacuum coffeemakers.*

The Different Coffeemakers and How They Work:
Drip Pot: This is the old-fashioned triple-decker pot; boiling water is poured into the upper compartment so that it trickles through the basket of grounds beneath into the pot below. *Tip:* For super-clear, fragrant coffee, scald pot with boiling water and line grounds basket with filter paper before adding grounds.
Percolator: Probably the most popular pot (many automatics are percolators). Grounds go

into a basket which stands on a tall, hollow stem inside the pot; the water goes into the pot proper and when it boils, bubbles up through the stem onto the grounds, then drips back into the pot below. Percolator tops have glass domes, the better to see the color of the coffee and the stage of doneness (when the coffee is deeply amber, it's done).
Vacuum Coffeemaker: An hour-glass-shaped pot, often automatic. Water goes into the lower compartment, grounds into the top (linked to the lower by a long spout). As the water boils, the upper compartment is fitted over the lower with a twist, insuring a tight fit so that steam will force the water up through the spout onto the grounds. After the water has steeped in the grounds 2-3 minutes, the heat is turned off and the coffee filters down into the lower chamber.

Coffee-Making Chart
(proportions apply to all grinds of coffee)

Servings	Coffee	Water
2	2 standard coffee measures*	1½ cups*
4	4 standard coffee measures	3 cups
6	6 standard coffee measures	4½ cups
8	8 standard coffee measures	6 cups
10	10 standard coffee measures	7½ cups
20	½ pound	1 gallon
40	1 pound	2 gallons
60	1½ pounds	3 gallons

* 1 standard coffee measure = 2 level measuring tablespoons; cups used are standard measuring cups.

About Making Coffee in Quantity: If you haven't a quantity pot, you can make coffee for a crowd this way, using proportions in chart as a guide: tie grounds in a muslin bag large enough to hold twice the amount you're putting into it, then immerse in a large kettle of boiling water, cover kettle, reduce heat and let grounds steep 10 to 12 minutes. Swish bag up and down several times in water to extract maximum flavor, then remove bag. For crystal clear coffee, add an egg shell or two to the kettle.

●

Cappuccino
For an extra fancy touch, sprinkle with nutmeg or cinnamon and top with whipped cream.
Makes 8 servings

3 cups boiling water
3 tablespoons instant espresso coffee
3 cups scalding hot milk

Pour boiling water over instant espresso coffee and stir until dissolved. Stir in hot milk and serve in mugs or tall, slim heat-proof glasses.
To Serve Cold: Chill coffee mixture well, pour

A coffee for every connoisseur no matter what his nationality—Italian, Irish, Austrian or American.

into tall slim glasses, top with sweetened whipped cream, sprinkle with cinnamon-sugar and serve with cinnamon stick stirrers.

●

Espresso Cream
After-dinner favorite goes Latin with chocolate and cinnamon.
Makes about 8 servings

2 cups water
9 squares (half a 4-ounce package) sweet cooking chocolate
1 three-inch piece stick cinnamon
2 tablespoons sugar
4 teaspoons instant espresso coffee
½ cup cream for whipping
Ground cinnamon

1 Combine water, chocolate, cinnamon stick, and sugar in a medium-size saucepan. Heat slowly, stirring constantly, until chocolate melts; stir in coffee until dissolved. Discard cinnamon stick.

2 Beat cream until stiff in a small bowl; spoon into demitasses; pour hot coffee mixture into each. Sprinkle with cinnamon. Serve hot.

●

Eggnog Brasilia
Punch-bowl perennial flavored with coffee, served warm for a change.
Makes 24 punch-cup servings

4 eggs, separated
3 cups milk
2 cups light cream or table cream
3 tablespoons instant coffee
½ cup light corn syrup
½ cup brandy
¼ cup water
Ground nutmeg

1 Beat egg yolks slightly in a large saucepan; stir in milk, cream, instant coffee, and ¼ cup of the corn syrup. Heat slowly, stirring often, to scalding; remove from heat. Stir in brandy.
2 Heat remaining ¼ cup corn syrup with water

107

to boiling in a small saucepan; simmer 5 minutes. Beat egg whites until foamy in a large bowl; slowly beat in hot syrup until meringue forms soft peaks; fold in egg-yolk mixture.

3 Pour or ladle into a punch bowl; sprinkle with nutmeg. Serve warm in punch cups or demitasses.

Irish Coffee

Serve in Irish coffee goblets or in mugs.
Makes 8 servings

8 teaspoons sugar
6 cups strong hot coffee
8 jiggers Irish whiskey
8 tablespoons whipped cream

1 Heat each goblet or mug by putting a metal spoon in the empty goblet and pouring hot water onto the spoon and then into the goblet. Pour out water.

2 Put a teaspoon of sugar in each goblet. Add enough coffee to dissolve the sugar; stir. Add a jigger of Irish whiskey to each goblet, then fill goblet to within an inch of the brim with more coffee.

3 Slide each spoonful of whipped cream over the back of a teaspoon held over each goblet of coffee. Do not stir. Serve at once.

Cafe Mexicano

Makes 4 servings

4 teaspoons chocolate syrup
½ cup cream for whipping
¼ teaspoon cinnamon (for topping)
¼ teaspoon nutmeg
1 tablespoon sugar
½ teaspoon cinnamon (for coffee)
1½ cups strong hot coffee

1 Put 1 teaspoon chocolate syrup into each of 4 small cups.

2 Combine heavy cream with ¼ teaspoon cinnamon, nutmeg, and sugar. Whip until stiff.

3 Stir ½ teaspoon cinnamon into coffee. Pour into cups and stir to blend with syrup. Top with spiced whipped cream.

108

Spiced Coffee Vienna

Makes 6 servings

3 cups extra-strong hot coffee
2 cinnamon sticks
4 whole cloves

4 allspice berries
Softly whipped cream
Nutmeg
Sugar

1 Pour coffee into chafing dish with a flame underneath it. Add cinnamon sticks, cloves, and allspice berries. Steep over very low heat for 10 to 15 minutes. Strain.

2 Pour into wine glasses and top with softly whipped cream. Sprinkle with nutmeg and serve with sugar.

Mediterranean Coffee

Makes 12 servings

2 quarts strong hot coffee
¼ cup chocolate syrup
⅓ cup sugar
4 cinnamon sticks, each about 3" long
1½ teaspoons whole cloves
½ teaspoon anise flavoring
Peel of 1 orange, in strips
Peel of 1 lemon, in strips
Whipped cream

1 Combine coffee, chocolate syrup, sugar, cinnamon, cloves, and anise in a deep chafing dish or a large carafe with a flame underneath it. Steep over very low heat for 15 minutes (do not boil).

2 Serve in demitasse cups or small mugs with a twist of lemon peel, a twist of orange peel, and a spoonful of whipped cream in each.

Orange Mocha

Cocoa mix adds to the appeal of this hot, hearty brew.
Makes 6 servings

1 small orange
6 cups freshly brewed strong coffee
1 cup instant cocoa mix
½ cup cream for whipping
1 tablespoon sugar
¼ teaspoon vanilla

1 Pare rind very thinly from orange with a vegetable parer. (Wrap fruit and save to use another time.)

2 Combine rind and coffee in a medium-size saucepan; simmer 5 minutes; remove rind and discard. Stir in cocoa mix until dissolved; remove from heat.

3 Beat cream with sugar and vanilla until stiff in a small bowl.

4 Pour coffee mixture into 6 mugs or large cups; float a generous spoonful of whipped cream on each. Serve hot.

For an unconventional cup of cheer, Eggnog Brazilia which is spiked and served hot.

BEVERAGES

Café Brûlot
Makes 8 servings

5 *lumps sugar*
1 *cup brandy*
1 *quart very strong hot coffee*
1 *stick cinnamon*
6 *cloves*
1 *piece vanilla bean*
3 *pieces orange rind*

1 Soak a sugar lump in brandy, remove, and set aside. Add remaining 4 sugar lumps to brandy.
2 Pour coffee into chafing dish or metal bowl with a flame underneath it. Add cinnamon, cloves, vanilla bean, and orange rind. Stir together. Add brandy.
3 Place the brandy-soaked lump of sugar on a serving ladle and ignite. Add, flaming, to the Café Brûlot and serve immediately.

Cognackaffe
Makes 12 servings

6 *eggs, chilled*
  Grated peel of 1 lemon
½ *cup sugar*
3 *cups cold strong coffee beverage*
⅔ *cup brandy or cognac*

1 Beat eggs and lemon peel until light and fluffy. Add sugar gradually and continue to beat until thick.
2 Stir in coffee slowly, then add brandy. Serve in chilled glasses.

Coffee Frappé
Try this dressy treat as a dinner beverage as well as an afternoon pickup.
Makes 4 servings

Café Brûlot, a bit of Creole pyrotechnics, is flamed just before serving, preferably in a darkened room.

110

2 tablespoons instant coffee
2 one-inch pieces stick cinnamon
3 cups hot water
   Few drops bottled aromatic bitters
   Sugar
¼ cup cream for whipping
2 teaspoons 10X (confectioners' powdered)
   sugar
   Crushed ice
   Grated orange rind

1 Combine instant coffee and cinnamon sticks in a 4-cup measure; add hot water and bitters. Sweeten to taste with sugar; cool.
2 When ready to serve, beat cream with 10X sugar until stiff in a small bowl.
3 Pour cooled coffee mixture over crushed ice in stemmed glasses, discarding cinnamon sticks. Top each with a generous spoonful of whipped cream; sprinkle with grated orange rind.

Carioca Fizz
Flavor is slightly bitter with just a hint of coffee.
Makes 2 servings

½ teaspoon instant coffee
½ teaspoon sweetened chocolate-flavor drink
   mix
½ teaspoon sugar
½ cup water
1 bottle (10 ounces) bitter-lemon carbonated
   beverage
4 orange slices
4 maraschino cherries

1 Combine instant coffee, chocolate-flavor drink mix, sugar, and water in a cup; stir until sugar dissolves.
2 Pour over ice in 2 tall glasses; fill with bitter-lemon beverage. Garnish each with orange slices and maraschino cherries threaded onto kebab sticks, as pictured.

Frosted Mocha
Freeze the coffee cubes ahead, and this tall creamy cooler goes together fast.
Makes 8 servings

8 tablespoons instant coffee
3 cups water
1 cup sweetened chocolate-flavor drink mix
¼ teaspoon ground cinnamon
4 cups milk
1 cup cream for whipping

1 Dissolve instant coffee in water in a 4-cup

Carioca Fizz

measure; pour into two ice-cube trays; freeze until firm.
2 When ready to serve, dissolve chocolate-flavor drink mix and cinnamon in milk in an 8-cup pitcher. Beat cream until stiff in a medium-size bowl; stir into milk mixture.
3 Place three or four coffee cubes in each of 8 tall glasses or mugs; pour milk mixture over top.

Brazilian Float
Go-steady flavors—chocolate and coffee—star in this rich creamy beverage.
Makes 4 servings

2 squares unsweetened chocolate
2 cups milk
⅓ cup sugar
2 cups freshly brewed double-strength coffee
1 pint coffee ice cream

1 Combine chocolate, milk, and sugar in a medium-size saucepan; heat slowly until chocolate melts; stir in coffee. Beat vigorously with a rotary beater until foamy; chill.
2 Pour into 4 tall glasses; float a scoop of ice cream on each. Garnish with chocolate curls,

111

if you wish. (To make, shave thin strips from a square of unsweetened chocolate with a vegetable parer or knife.)

TEA

Tips on Buying:

Perfect tea, like perfect coffee, is a blend of 20 to 30 different varieties. Although all teas come from the same plant, soil, climate and manufacturing processes account for the flavor and color differences we know. Basically, all teas fall into three classes: *black, green* and *oolong*. Most familiar of all is black tea—a rich, fermented blend, usually of orange pekoe and pekoe to brew for either hot or iced tea. Green tea has a much lighter color and more delicate flavor and is best served hot. Oolong—neither black nor green—is best described as halfway between the two and makes a distinctive, sweet, amber brew.

When you shop for tea, take time to look over the items your supermarket offers. You'll find loose teas in four, six and eight-ounce cartons or tins; tea bags in regular and king size; instant tea in glass jars, and specialty products flavored or scented with mint, orange peel or spices. Iced-tea mixes, presweetened or artificially sweetened, with mint or lemon, come prepackaged in single-serving or family-size envelopes. During the summer your dairy case even holds ready-made iced tea to pour right from carton or jar.

Tips on Storing:

Store tea in a tightly covered container in a cool spot to protect its freshness.

Tips for Making Perfect Tea:

Perfect tea is honey-hued and clear. It is fragrant without being astringent or bitter, fairly robust but not overpowering. To make it:
• Rinse teapot with boiling water, then drain.
• Use fresh, top quality tea and freshly drawn soft water.
• Measure carefully, allowing for each serving 1 cup freshly boiling water and 1 tea bag or 1 teaspoon loose tea. *Note: When making iced tea,* use half again as much tea; the ice will dilute the tea.
• Allow tea to steep 3 to 5 minutes, then serve with sugar and lemon or milk.

About Making Hot Tea in Quantity: The best way is to make a strong tea concentrate beforehand. At serving time, you simply pour about 2 tablespoons of the concentrate into each cup, then dilute with hot water. *To Make Tea Concentrate* (enough for 40-45 cups tea): Bring 1½ quarts water to a boil, remove from heat and add ¼ pound loose tea; stir, cover, let steep 5 minutes, then strain into a teapot.

About Making Iced Tea in Quantity: The principle is the same as for making hot tea in quantity, that is, you prepare a concentrate, then water it down. *To Make Tea Concentrate* (enough for 20 servings): Pour 1 quart boiling water over ⅔ cup loose tea, stir, cover and let steep 6 minutes. Strain concentrate into 3 quarts cold water. Tea is now the proper strength to serve.
Tip: Whenever iced tea clouds (refrigeration makes it go murky), clear by adding a little boiling water. The best preventive is simply to keep tea at room temperature and to pour into ice-filled glasses.

Apricot-Orange Tea

Fruit juices and spice enliven hot tea in a pair of cold-weather warmers.
Makes 6 servings

    2 ½ cups apricot nectar
      1 cup orange juice
      1 cup water
      1 tablespoon sugar
      1 teaspoon ground cinnamon
      4 lemon slices
     12 whole cloves
      2 teaspoons instant tea

1 Combine apricot nectar, orange juice, water, sugar, and cinnamon in a medium-size saucepan. Insert 3 cloves into each lemon slice; add to saucepan.
2 Heat just to boiling; reduce heat; cover. Simmer 5 minutes. Stir in tea. Serve hot.

CRAN-ORANGE TEA—Combine 2½ cups cranberry-juice cocktail, 1 cup orange juice, 1 cup water, ⅓ cup sugar, 2 broken cinnamon sticks, 2 quartered orange slices, and ⅛ teaspoon nutmeg in a medium-size saucepan. Heat just to boiling; reduce heat; cover. Simmer 5 minutes. Stir in 2 teaspoons instant tea. Serve hot. Makes 6 servings.

Tea Sparkle

When you want to fuss, frost the rims of glasses with lemon sugar.
Makes 6 servings

      6 regular-size tea bags
      3 cups freshly boiling water
      1 bottle (28 ounces) lemon-lime-flavor carbonated beverage
        Ice cubes

1 Place tea bags in a teapot; pour over freshly

Particularly welcome at a winter party is Apricot-Orange Tea. Make it good and spicy, serve it good and hot.

boiling water; brew 3 to 5 minutes. Pour into a large pitcher; let stand at room temperature to cool. Stir in carbonated beverage.

2 Pour over ice cubes in tall glasses.

NOTE: To frost rims of glasses, mix 2 tablespoons sugar and 1 teaspoon grated lemon rind in a saucedish. Beat 1 egg white slightly in a small bowl. Dip rims of glasses in egg white, then into sugar mixture to coat generously; let stand until sugar dries.

Dapple Apple Flip

Tea blends with apple juice for this delightful thirst quencher.
Makes 8 servings

6 regular-size tea bags
3 cups freshly boiling water
1 quart apple juice
2 tablespoons lemon juice
  Sugar
  Ice cubes

1 Place tea bags in a teapot; pour over freshly boiling water; brew 3 to 5 minutes. Pour into a large pitcher; let stand at room temperature to cool.

2 Stir in apple juice and lemon juice; sweeten to taste with sugar.

3 Pour over ice cubes in tall glasses. Garnish each with a lemon wedge, if you wish.

MILK DRINKS

4 Jiffy Milk Drinks
Each makes 1 serving

• CHOCOLATE MILK: Blend 2 tablespoons chocolate syrup or cocoa mix with 1 cup milk.
• VANILLA MILK: Blend 2 teaspoons sugar and ½ teaspoon vanilla with 1 cup milk.
• CARAMEL MILK: Heat 1 cup milk with 2 tablespoons light brown sugar until sugar is dissolved. Stir in ¼ teaspoon vanilla. Serve hot or cold.
• MILK AND HONEY: Stir 1 to 2 tablespoons honey into 1 cup milk, sprinkle lightly with nutmeg or cinnamon.

Choco-Mint Milk
Favorite chocolate is sparked with cooling mint.
Makes 4 servings

1 quart milk
½ cup cocoa mix
¼ teaspoon peppermint extract
  Whipped cream from a pressurized can
  Fresh mint sprigs

1 Combine milk, cocoa mix, and mint extract in container of electric blender. Whirl at high speed until smooth.

2 To serve, pour into 4 tall glasses; top with swirl of whipped cream; garnish each glass with a sprig of mint.

Banana Smoothie
Here's a honey of a way to cater to a sweet tooth.
Makes 4 servings

2 cups milk
2 large ripe bananas, peeled and sliced
¼ cup honey
½ teaspoon vanilla

1 Combine all ingredients in an electric-blender container; cover; whirl until foamy-thick. (Or place in a 4-cup measure and beat with rotary beater.)

2 Pour into mugs or tumblers.

Pink Moo
Raspberry syrup and milk make this child's-delight hot beverage.
Makes 4 servings

1 quart milk
½ cup bottled raspberry syrup
  Red food coloring

1 Combine milk and raspberry syrup in a medium-size saucepan; tint rosy-pink with food coloring. Heat slowly, just until tiny bubbles form around edge of pan.

2 Pour into mugs or cups; top with a fluff of whipped cream from a pressurized can, if you wish.

Purple Cow
Grape juice blended with milk makes a drink that's high in energy.
Makes 4 servings

114

2 cups milk
1 cup bottled grape juice
1 pint vanilla ice cream

1 Combine milk, grape juice, and half the ice cream in container of electric blender. Whirl at high speed until thick and foamy.
2 To serve, pour into 4 tall glasses. Top with remaining ice cream, dividing evenly. Garnish with whipped cream from a pressurized can and maraschino cherries, if you wish.
PINK COW—Prepare above recipe, substituting bottled cranberry juice cocktail for grape juice.

Cider Syllabub
Makes 12 punch-cup servings

1 ¼ cups sugar
  3 cups apple cider
  3 tablespoons grated lemon rind
  ¼ cup lemon juice
  1 teaspoon light corn syrup
  ½ teaspoon bottled aromatic bitters
  2 egg whites
  2 cups milk
  1 cup light cream or table cream

1 Combine 1 cup of the sugar, cider, lemon rind and juice, corn syrup, and bitters in a large bowl; stir until sugar dissolves. Chill several hours, or until frosty-cold.
2 Just before serving, beat egg whites until foamy-white in a small bowl; beat in remaining ¼ cup sugar, 1 tablespoon at a time, until meringue stands in firm peaks.
3 Beat milk and cream into cider mixture until frothy; pour into a punch bowl. Spoon meringue in small puffs on top. Serve in punch cups, floating meringue on each.

Spicy Fruit Lowball
The zippy buttermilk flavor makes this an especially refreshing drink.
Makes 6 servings

1 package (10 ounces) frozen peaches
¼ cup firmly packed light brown sugar
¼ teaspoon ground cinnamon
1 quart buttermilk
1 medium navel orange

1 Thaw peaches, following package directions.
2 Combine peaches, brown sugar, and cinnamon in container of electric blender. Whirl at medium speed until smooth; add buttermilk; whirl to mix.
3 To serve, pour into six 8-ounce glasses. Cut orange into very thin slices; garnish each serving with a slice of orange on edge of glass. Top with a dash of cinnamon, if you wish.

Buttermilk Float
Your blender whips up this tangy-sweet drink in a hurry.
Makes 4 servings

3 cups buttermilk
1 pint lemon sherbet
  Cinnamon-sugar

1 Combine buttermilk and about half of the sherbet in an electric-blender container; cover. Beat until smooth. (Or place in a 4-cup measure and beat with rotary beater.)
2 Pour into 4 tall glasses; top each with a spoonful of the remaining sherbet. Sprinkle with cinnamon-sugar.

Cocoa
Makes 4 to 6 servings

  3 tablespoons dry cocoa
  ¼ cup sugar
  1 quart milk
  ¼ teaspoon vanilla
  4 marshmallows

1 Blend cocoa and sugar.
2 Heat milk to scalding; mix a little hot milk into cocoa mixture, then add to hot milk and stir until well blended. Add vanilla, pour into cups or mugs and float a marshmallow in each.

115

Old-Fashioned Hot Chocolate
Makes 4 to 6 servings

  2 squares unsweetened chocolate
  ⅓ cup sugar
  1 quart milk
    Pinch salt
  ½ teaspoon vanilla

1 Place all ingredients except vanilla in a medium-size saucepan and heat and stir until chocolate is melted and mixture smooth and uniformly chocolate brown.
2 Add vanilla, pour into cups and serve.
Tip: For extra rich hot chocolate, use half evaporated milk or light cream and half regular milk.

Mexican Hot Chocolate
Makes 6 servings

1 quart milk
3 squares semisweet chocolate
1 teaspoon ground cinnamon
2 eggs

1 Heat milk just to scalding in a large saucepan. Stir in chocolate and cinnamon until chocolate melts, then beat with a rotary beater until smooth.
2 Beat eggs well in a small bowl; slowly beat in about 1 cup of the hot chocolate mixture, then beat back into remaining chocolate mixture in pan. Heat slowly, stirring constantly, 1 minute; beat again until frothy.
3 Ladle into heated mugs or glasses; place a cinnamon stick in each mug for a stirrer, if you wish. Serve warm.

Mocha Au Lait
Café au lait two ways—one flavored chocolate, one flavored coconut.
Makes 4 servings

¼ cup dry cocoa (not cocoa mix)
6 tablespoons sugar
1 quart milk
3 tablespoons freeze-dried coffee
½ teaspoon vanilla

1 Blend cocoa and sugar in a large saucepan; stir in ½ cup of the milk to make a smooth paste; gradually add remaining milk, stirring constantly. Heat, stirring often, until piping-hot. (Do not boil.)
2 Add coffee and vanilla, stirring until coffee is dissolved. Serve hot.
  CARIBBEAN AU LAIT—Combine 1 quart milk with ½ cup flaked coconut in a large saucepan. Heat until piping-hot. (Do not boil.) Strain milk; discard coconut. Stir ¼ cup sugar, 2 tablespoons freeze-dried coffee, and ¼ teaspoon ground cinnamon into hot milk until sugar is dissolved (reheat if necessary). Serve hot. Makes 4 servings.

Hot Buttered Milk
Children—and grownups, too—will go for this warmer-upper on a blustery day
Makes 4 to 6 servings

1 quart milk
⅓ cup firmly packed light brown sugar
4 tablespoons (½ stick) butter or margarine
  Nutmeg

1 Combine milk, brown sugar, and butter or margarine in a medium-size saucepan. Heat slowly, stirring constantly, just until butter or margarine melts. (Do not let milk boil.)
2 Pour into mugs or cups; sprinkle with nutmeg.

FRUIT DRINKS

Old-Fashioned Lemonade
Makes 6 servings

1 ¼ cups sugar
1 cup water
  Peel of 2 lemons, cut in strips and bitter white part removed
1 cup fresh or bottled lemon juice
4 cups ice water

1 Gently boil sugar, 1 cup water and lemon peel in a small saucepan 8 to 10 minutes until sugar is dissolved and mixture syrupy; remove lemon peel and cool to room temperature.
2 Pour syrup into a large pitcher, add lemon juice and ice water and stir well. Add plenty of ice cubes and stir well again. Serve in tall glasses.
To Make Pink Lemonade: Prepare lemonade as directed and mix in 3 tablespoons bottled grenadine.
To Make Old-Fashioned Limeade: Prepare as for Old-Fashioned Lemonade, substituting lime peel and lime juice for the lemon peel and lemon juice.

Old-Fashioned Orangeade
Makes 6 to 8 servings

1 cup sugar
1 cup water
  Peel of 1 orange and 1 lemon, cut in strips and bitter white part removed

Old-Fashioned Limeade, Cherry Cheerer, Fruit Swizzle and cream-topped cola are a cool summer foursome.

116

¼ cup fresh or bottled lemon juice
2 cups fresh, frozen or canned orange juice
3 cups ice water

1 Gently boil sugar, 1 cup water, lemon and orange peels in a small saucepan 8 to 10 minutes until sugar dissolves and mixture is syrupy; remove peels and cool syrup to room temperature.
2 Pour syrup into a large pitcher, add remaining ingredients and mix well. Add plenty of ice cubes and stir to chill. Serve over ice in tall glasses.

Grapefruit Fizz
Flavor is spicy yet tangy. And it's so refreshing on a hot day.
Makes 6 servings

1 cup sugar
2 cups water
3 whole allspice
3 whole cloves
1 can (6 ounces) frozen concentrated grapefruit juice
1 bottle (28 ounces) ginger ale
Green food coloring
Ice cubes
1 lemon, cut in 6 slices
6 maraschino cherries

1 Combine sugar, water, allspice, and cloves in a medium-size saucepan; heat to boiling, then simmer 5 minutes. Strain into a large pitcher; cool.
2 Stir in frozen grapefruit juice until thawed, then ginger ale and a few drops food coloring to tint green.
3 Pour over ice cubes in 6 tall glasses; garnish each with a slice of lemon and a maraschino cherry.

Orange Blush
Fruit-flavor drink mix is your starter for this pitcher-mixed refresher.
Makes 6 servings

1 envelope (about 3 ounces) sweetened orangeade mix
1 can (12 ounces) apricot nectar, chilled
1 tablespoon lemon juice
6 orange slices

Prepare orangeade mix, following label directions; stir in apricot nectar and lemon juice. Pour into 6 tall glasses. Garnish each with an orange slice.

Lemon Blush
Makes 6 servings

1 6-ounce can frozen concentrate for lemonade
12 teaspoons bottled grenadine or raspberry syrup
6 maraschino cherries

1 Prepare lemonade concentrate in a large pitcher following label directions; add ice.
2 Pour into 6 tall glasses. Carefully pour 2 teaspoons grenadine or raspberry down inside each glass to give a two-tone effect. Garnish with maraschino cherries.

Lemon 'n' Lime Ade
Makes 8 to 10 servings

2 cups sugar
4 cups water
½ cup bottled lemon juice
½ cup bottled lime juice
2 bottles (12 ounces each) ginger ale
8 to 10 mint sprigs

1 Heat and stir sugar and water in a medium-size saucepan just until sugar is dissolved; cool to lukewarm.
2 Stir in lemon and lime juices and pour into a large pitcher. Mix in ginger ale, pour into tall glasses filled with ice and sprig with mint.

Fruit Swizzle
Makes 8 servings

1 can (6 ounces) frozen concentrate for lemonade
1 can (6 ounces) frozen concentrated orange juice
Water
16 strawberries
8 lime wedges

1 Mix frozen concentrates in an 8-cup measure; add water to total 4 cups and stir well. Fill with ice cubes, cover and chill.
2 To serve, place 2 strawberries and 1 lime wedge in each of 8 tall glasses; pour in fruit swizzle.

West Coast Cooler
Makes 8 to 10 servings

1 can (6 ounces) frozen concentrate for
   strawberry-lemon punch
3 cups water
2 bottles (12 ounces each) orange-flavor soda

Combine all ingredients in a large pitcher; pour
over ice cubes in tall glasses.

Cypress Fling
Makes 8 to 10 servings

1 can (6 ounces) frozen concentrated
   pineapple-orange juice
1 ½ cups water
1 can (12 ounces) apricot nectar
1 bottle (28 ounces) lemon-lime-flavor carbonated beverage

Combine all ingredients in a large pitcher; pour
over ice cubes in tall glasses.

Cherry Cheerer
Makes 4 to 6 servings

1 envelope cherry-flavor soft-drink crystals
1 26-ounce bottle cola beverage

Combine ingredients in a large pitcher, stirring
until all drink crystals are dissolved. Pour over
ice in tall glasses.

Cranberry Mist
Makes 6 servings

1 can (about 1 pint 2 ounces) pineapple juice
1 16-ounce bottle cranberry juice cocktail
   Lemon slices to garnish

Mix pineapple juice and cranberry juice cocktail
in a large pitcher, pour over crushed ice in tall
glasses and garnish with lemon slices.

Mulled Cranberry Juice
Cranberry juice and cider, spiced just right,
make this peppy warm beverage.
Makes 8 servings

1 bottle (1 quart) cranberry juice cocktail
2 cups apple cider
¼ cup golden raisins
5 whole cloves
5 whole allspice

To make Lemon 'N Lime Ade visually cool, tint green.

1 Combine cranberry juice cocktail, cider, and
raisins in a medium-size saucepan. Tie cloves
and allspice in a cheesecloth bag and add to
pan.
2 Heat slowly, 5 minutes, or just until warm;
remove spice bag.

119

3 Ladle into stemmed glasses, adding some of the raisins to each; garnish each with an orange slice threaded onto a cinnamon stick, if you wish.

●

Strawberry Spree
Sparkly grenadine syrup forms a rosy layer in the bottom of each glass.
Makes 4 servings

1 pint strawberry ice cream
2 cups milk
8 teaspoons bottled grenadine syrup
  Whole strawberries

1 Beat ice cream and milk until foamy-thick in an electric blender or 4-cup measure; pour into 4 tall glasses.
2 Pour 2 teaspoons grenadine syrup from a spoon down inside of each glass. (It will run to bottom to make a rosy layer.) Garnish each with 3 strawberries threaded onto a kebab stick.

Raspberry Sparkle

Strawberry Spree

Raspberry Sparkle
Weight-watchers: Sip with a clear conscience, for each glass is just 18 calories.
Makes 4 servings

3 envelopes (3 to a package) low-calorie raspberry-flavor gelatin
2 cups hot water
2 cups cold water
3 tablespoons lime juice
  Ice cubes
  Lime wedges

1 Dissolve gelatin in hot water in a pitcher; stir in cold water and lime juice. Pour over ice cubes in 4 tall glasses.
2 Garnish each with lime wedges threaded onto a kebab stick.

PARTY PUNCHES

Apricot Mist
Makes about 50 punch-cup servings

1 can (46 ounces) apricot nectar
1 can (46 ounces) pineapple juice
3 cans (6 ounces each) frozen concentrate for
  limeade
3 bottles (28 ounces each) ginger ale

120

Combine apricot nectar, pineapple juice, and concentrate for limeade in a punch bowl; stir in ginger ale. Add ice cubes; float a few lime slices and whole strawberries on top, if you wish.

Double Raspberry Frost
Makes about 25 punch-cup servings

1 cup bottled raspberry syrup
2 cups water
2 cans (6 ounces each) frozen concentrate for lemonade
2 bottles (28 ounces each) raspberry-flavor carbonated beverage

Stir raspberry syrup into water in a punch bowl, then stir in concentrate for lemonade and carbonated beverage. Add ice cubes; float a few lemon slices and sprigs of mint on top, if you wish.

Ceylon Fizz
Makes about 14 punch-cup servings

1 cup orange juice
2 cups water
½ cup lemon juice
½ cup sugar
4 teaspoons instant powdered tea
2 bottles (7 ounces each) lemon-lime-flavor carbonated beverage

Combine orange juice, water, lemon juice, sugar, and instant tea in a punch bowl; stir until sugar and tea dissolve, then stir in carbonated beverage. Add ice cubes; float a few orange slices on top, if you wish.

Wikiwiki Punch
True to its name, it's ready about as fast as you can flip the lids from bottles.
Makes 16 large punch-cup servings

3 cans (6 ounces each) frozen concentrate for lemonade, thawed
2 bottles (about 28 ounces each) ginger ale
2 bottles (about 28 ounces each) quinine water
1 cup bottled grenadine syrup
Ice
½ lemon, sliced
½ lime, sliced
Fresh mint

1 Combine concentrate for lemonade, ginger ale, quinine water, and grenadine syrup in a large bowl.

Add a large *Ice Mold* (*directions below*) or several trays of ice.
2 Thread each lemon and lime slice with a sprig of mint; float on top. Serve in paper cups.
Ice Mold—The day before your party, fill a 6- or 8-cup mold with water; freeze until firm. To remove from mold, dip *very quickly* in and out of a pan of hot water; invert onto a plate, then add to punch bowl.

Cider Cup
Go festive and make a colorful Orange Ice Ring to float in your punch bowl.
Makes about 30 punch-cup servings

Orange Ice Ring (directions follow)
8 cups apple cider
1 can (9 ounces) frozen concentrate for imitation orange juice
1 cup light corn syrup
1 bottle (28 ounces) ginger ale
Mint sprigs

1 One or two days ahead, make *Orange Ice Ring** so it will be frozen firm.
2 Combine cider, imitation orange juice, and corn syrup in a large pitcher. Chill at least 3 hours.
3 Just before serving, pour mixture into a punch bowl; stir in ginger ale. Add ice ring. Garnish with a few sprigs of mint.
Orange Ice Ring—Thinly slice 1 small seedless orange; arrange slices in a circle in a 5-cup ring mold. Pour in ½ cup water; freeze until firm. Add enough cold water to fill mold; freeze. To remove from mold, dip mold *very quickly* in and out of hot water; invert onto a plate.

Cranberry-Lemon Frost
Scoops of sherbet add creaminess and a pleasing tang to this party refresher.
Makes about 18 punch-cup servings

1 bottle (32 ounces) cranberry juice cocktail
2 cans (12 ounces each) apricot nectar
½ cup light corn syrup
1 pint lemon sherbet
Mint sprigs

1 Combine cranberry juice cocktail, apricot nectar, and corn syrup in a large pitcher. Chill at least 3 hours.
2 Just before serving, pour mixture into a punch bowl. Scoop or spoon lemon sherbet into small balls; float on top. Garnish with a cluster of mint.
Tip: If you have a freezer, save yourself last-

121

minute fussing by shaping ice-cream balls ahead. Place in a single layer on a cooky sheet; cover with transparent wrap; freeze until serving time.

Spiced Peach Punch
Makes 12 servings

1 46-ounce can peach nectar
1 20-ounce can orange juice
½ cup firmly packed brown sugar
3 three-inch pieces stick cinnamon, broken
½ teaspoon whole cloves
2 tablespoons bottled lime juice

1 Combine peach nectar, orange juice, and brown sugar in a large saucepan. Tie cinnamon and cloves in a small cheesecloth bag; drop into saucepan.
2 Heat slowly, stirring constantly, until sugar dissolves; simmer 10 minutes. Stir in lime juice.
3 Ladle into mugs. Garnish each with thin strips of orange rind threaded onto cinnamon sticks, if you wish. Serve warm.

Hot Mulled Cider
Makes 16 servings

4 quarts apple cider
1 cup firmly-packed brown sugar
9 whole cloves

Spiced Peach Punch is perfect for winter warm-ups.

9 whole allspice
4 cinnamon sticks, broken into 1-inch pieces
2 lemons, thinly sliced

Tie cloves, allspice and cinnamon in a cheesecloth bag; place in a large kettle with cider and sugar; simmer 5 minutes. Just before serving, remove spice bag. Serve in mugs, and float a lemon slice in each.

Claret Cup
Makes about 25 punch-cup servings

½ cup Curaçao liqueur
1 can (46 ounces) lemon pink Hawaiian punch, chilled
1 bottle (4/5 quart) claret, chilled
1 bottle (1 pint, 10 ounces) lemon-lime carbonated beverage, chilled
   Ice ring (recipes follow)
1 orange, cut into thin slices

1 Mix Curaçao and punch in bowl.
2 Just before serving, add claret and carbonated beverage; carefully slide in *Ice Ring*   and add orange slices.
   CLEAR ICE RING—Fill a 6- or 8-cup ring mold with water; set in freezer for 4 hours, or overnight, or until frozen solid. To unmold, let stand at room temperature about 5 minutes, or until Ice ring is movable in mold. Invert onto a cooky sheet and slide carefully into filled punch bowl.
   STRAWBERRY ICE RING—Pour water to a depth of ¼ inch into a 6- or 8-cup ring mold; freeze about 20 minutes, or until firm. Arrange about 8 whole strawberries on top of frozen layer; pour in ¾ cup water; freeze. To keep berries in place, keep adding water, a little at a time, freezing after each addition, until mold is filled. Freeze until solid. To unmold, let stand at room temperature about 5 minutes, or until Ice ring is movable in mold. Invert onto a cooky sheet and slide carefully into filled punch bowl.

Celebration Punch
Makes about 25 punch-cup servings

½ cup light corn syrup
½ cup brandy
1 bottle (4/5 quart) sauterne, chilled
1 bottle (28 ounces) carbonated water, chilled
1 bottle (4/5 quart) champagne, chilled
   Ice cubes or Ice ring
2 cups (1 pint) whole strawberries, washed (not hulled)

1 Mix corn syrup and brandy in punch bowl until well-blended; stir in sauterne.

Mulled Wine Punch, if not steamy-hot, can be served from a decorative frosted or cut glass punch bowl.

2 Just before serving, add carbonated water and champagne. Carefully add ice cubes or slide in ice ring; add strawberries.

●

Daiquiri Punch
Makes about 25 punch-cup servings

½ cup light corn syrup
2 cups light rum
2 cans (6 ounces each) frozen daiquiri mix,
   thawed
2 bottles (28 ounces each) carbonated water,
   chilled
   Ice ring
1 lime, cut into thin slices

1 Mix corn syrup and rum in punch bowl, stirring to blend; stir in daiquiri mix.
2 Just before serving, add carbonated water, then carefully slide in ice ring and add lime slices.

●

Mulled Wine Punch
Makes about 15 punch-cup servings

1 bottle (1 quart) cranberry juice cocktail
½ cup granulated sugar
½ cup firmly packed light brown sugar
½ stick cinnamon
6 whole cloves

6 whole allspice
1 bottle (4/5 quart) Burgundy

1 Mix cranberry juice and sugars in a large saucepan. Tie spices in a square of cheesecloth and add to saucepan; heat to boiling, uncovered; reduce heat; simmer 5 minutes. Discard spice bag.
2 Add Burgundy; heat until piping-hot (*do not boil*). Ladle into heatproof pitcher for serving. To keep hot, serve in mugs.

Coffee Punch Parisienne
Makes 16 punch-cup servings

3 cups regular strength coffee
2 cups apple juice
1 cup apricot brandy
¼ teaspoon ground ginger
2 bottles (7 ounces each) ginger ale

1 Combine coffee, apple juice, brandy, and ginger in a large saucepan. Heat slowly just to simmering; remove from heat.
2 Stir in ginger ale. Ladle into heated small mugs or punch cups. Serve warm.

Hot Tea Nectar
Makes 30 servings

8 cups boiling water
8 regular-size tea bags
1 can (18 ounces) unsweetened pineapple juice
1 can (12 ounces) apricot nectar
1 can (6 ounces) frozen concentrate for orange juice
1 can (6 ounces) frozen lemon juice
1 cup sugar
2 ¼ cups water

1 Pour boiling water over tea bags in a kettle; cover. Steep 5 minutes; remove tea bags.
2 Combine pineapple juice, apricot nectar, orange concentrate, lemon juice, sugar, and water in a kettle; heat slowly, stirring several times, to simmering. Stir in hot tea.
3 Very carefully pour into a large punch bowl. Garnish with lime and lemon slices and maraschino cherries threaded onto a long skewer, if you wish. Ladle into punch cups. Serve warm.

Plantation Eggnog
Makes 20 punch-cup servings

9 eggs
1 cup very fine granulated sugar

2 cups bourbon
½ cup cognac
2 cups light cream or table cream
3 cups cream for whipping
Grated nutmeg

1 Separate eggs, placing yolks in a large bowl and whites in a second large bowl.
2 Add sugar to egg yolks; beat until fluffy-thick. Stir in bourbon, cognac, and light cream. Chill several hours, or until very cold.
3 Beat egg whites until they stand in firm peaks. Beat cream until stiff in a large bowl. Fold beaten egg whites, then whipped cream into egg-yolk mixture; pour into a large punch bowl. Sprinkle with grated nutmeg. Ladle into punch cups.

Wassail Bowl
Makes 25 punch-cup servings

12 small red apples
3 whole cloves
3 whole allspice
3 cardamom seeds, coarsely broken
1 three-inch piece stick cinnamon, broken
2 bottles (1 quart each) ale
1 teaspoon ground ginger
1 teaspoon ground nutmeg
2 cups sugar
1 bottle (4/5 quart) dry sherry
6 eggs, separated

1 Place apples in a shallow baking pan. Bake in moderate oven (350°) 20 minutes, or until tender but still firm enough to hold their shape. Set aside.
2 Tie cloves, allspice, cardamom seeds, and cinnamon in a small double-thick cheesecloth bag. Place in a kettle with 2 cups of the ale, ginger, and nutmeg. Heat very slowly 10 minutes; remove spice bag. Stir in remaining ale, sugar, and sherry. Heat slowly 20 minutes. (Do not boil.)
3 Beat egg whites until they stand in firm peaks in a large bowl. Beat egg yolks well in a second large bowl; fold in egg whites. Slowly beat in hot ale mixture until smooth.
4 Very carefully pour into a large punch bowl; float baked apples on top. Ladle into heated mugs or punch cups. Serve warm.

Taken from the top, Claret Cup, Celebration Punch with a flotilla of strawberries, and Cider Cup.

BEVERAGES

Glogg
Makes 12 punch-cup servings

1 bottle (4/5 quart) dry red wine
½ cup seedless raisins
   Thin rind from ½ orange
8 whole cloves
1 half-inch piece stick cinnamon
10 cardamom seeds, coarsely broken
1 bottle (4/5 quart) aquavit
10 pieces loaf sugar
   Whole blanched almonds

1 Combine wine and raisins in a large saucepan. Tie orange rind, cloves, cinnamon, and cardamom seeds in a small double-thick cheesecloth bag. Add to saucepan; cover. Heat very slowly just to simmering; simmer 15 minutes. (Do not boil.) Remove spice bag.
2 Heat aquavit slowly in a medium-size saucepan.
3 Place sugar in a large chafing dish. Pour about ½ cup of the hot aquavit over top. Ignite with a match; let stand until sugar dissolves. Stir in hot wine mixture and remaining aquavit.
4 Ladle into heated punch cups, adding a few raisins and one or two almonds to each serving. Serve warm.

INDEX TO RECIPES IN THIS VOLUME

127

Beverages:

128